STORY JOURNEY

Thomas E. Boomershine

STORY JOURNEY

AN INVITATION
TO THE GOSPEL AS STORYTELLING

Abingdon Press
Nashville

Story Journey: An Invitation to the Gospel as Storytelling

Copyright © 1988 by Thomas E. Boomershine

This book is printed on recycled acid-free paper,

Library of Congress Cataloging-in-Publication Data

BOOMERSHINE, THOMAS E.
  Story journey: an invitation to the Gospel as storytelling / Thomas E. Boomershine.
  p. cm.
  Bibliography: p.
  Includes index.
ISBN 0-687-39662-X (alk. paper)
  1. Bible. N.T. Gospels—Reading. 2. Bible. N.T. Gospels—Use. 3. Storytelling. 4. Story-telling (Christian theology) I. Title.
BS2555.5.B66   1988   88-19038
226'.066—dc19

Except where otherwise indicated, Scripture quotations are from the Revised Standard Version of the Bible, copyright 1946, 1952, 1971 by the Division of Christian Education of the National Council of Churches of Christ in the U.S.A. Used by permission. Adaptations in the RSV text have been made in places by the author, in consultation with the Greek New Testament. Italics also added in places by the author.

Scripture quotations marked "author's trans." are original translations from the Greek.

The scripture quotation marked "RSV Apocrypha" is from the Revised Standard Version Apocrypha, copyright 1957 by the Division of Christian Education of the National Council of the Churches of Christ in the U.S.A. Used by permission.

Scripture quotations marked NIV are from the *Holy Bible: New International Version.* Copyright © 1973, 1978, 1984 by the International Bible Society. Used by permission of Zondervan Bible Publishers.

97 98 99 00 01 02 03 — 10 9

MANUFACTURED IN THE UNITED STATES OF AMERICA

To my father and mother,
Glenn and Garnet Boomershine

Contents

Preface and Acknowledgments..................................... 9

Beginnings... 15

1. **Birth** (Luke 2:1-20).. 23
   Learning the Story Alone

2. **Baptism** (Mark 1:9-13)................................... 41
   Learning the Story with a Friend

3. **Healing a Paralytic** (Mark 2:1-13)..................... 53
   Teaching the Story to Others

4. **The Prodigal Son** (Luke 15:11-32)..................... 69
   Listening to a Story as a Story

5. **Walking on the Water** (Matthew 14:22-33)......... 93
   The Story in Prayer and Pastoral Care

6. **A Syro-Phoenician Woman** (Mark 7:24-30)........ 107
   The Story in Peacemaking

7. **Bartimaeus** (Mark 10:46-52)............................ 123
   The Story in Preaching

8. **The Last Supper** (Mark 14:17-25)..................... 143
   The Story in Religious Education

9. **Crucifixion** (Mark 15:21-41)............................ 159

10. **Resurrection** (Mark 16:1-8)............................ 179

   Endings.. 197

   Appendix... 205

   Works Cited.. 209

   Selected Bibliography.................................... 210

   Index.. 213

   Scripture Index... 217

PREFACE
AND
ACKNOWLEDGMENTS

The best way to tell you about this book is to ask you to think of it as a large, clear woodland pool fed by deep, subterranean springs and several bubbling brooks. Identifying the springs and streams that flow into this pool may help prospective swimmers decide whether they want to try these waters. As in biblical genealogies, many names appear here, some of which may not be widely known. But each name is important and is connected with a much longer story, in which many other persons were involved who remain unnamed or even unknown, but not forgotten.

The stream of biblical scholarship is the deep spring that provides the clear, cool water in this pool. This book began with James Muilenburg's telling the Yahwist's story of creation from Genesis 2–3 during a lecture at Union Theological Seminary. J. Louis Martyn, Samuel Terrien, Amos Wilder, Hermann Gunkel, Rudolph Bultmann, and Martin Dibelius have taught me, in distinctive ways, how to swim in this bracing water. Gil Bartholomew, David Rhoads, and Merrill Miller have, as scholarly colleagues and friends, shared the deep dives of exploring the gospel as storytelling.

Another deep spring is contemporary literary criticism and,

in particular, Wayne Booth, with whom I studied at Earlham College. I will never forget working with him in the reading room of the British Museum as he was checking the proofs for *The Rhetoric of Fiction.* His teaching and work have enabled me to understand the logic and structure of narrative.

Still another major spring for this pool has been the media research associated with the name of Marshall McLuhan. In the subsequent work of Walter Ong and Werner Kelber, the radical nature of the shift from the world of orality to the world of literacy has been made clear. This work has in turn enabled me to understand the shape of oral experience and what is needed for literate persons to enter the world of storytelling.

Over to the left is the sparkling, wide stream of the storytelling tradition. Listening to the rich storytelling traditions of black preaching proved to me that long biblical stories could have great energy and life. Robert Newbold and James Forbes have shown me the way to that stream. The traditions of Jewish storytelling, from Martin Buber to Elie Wiesel and Rabbi David Dinn, have enabled me to hear the stories of the Gospels in the context of the storytellers of Israel. In that same storytelling stream are the contemporary storytellers who have been vital contributors to the renaissance of storytelling, in particular Ken Feit, Jay O'Callahan, and Bill White.

On the other side of the big tree is the stream of experiential approaches to biblical study. Walter Wink and I have shared a common quest for a new pattern of relationship between biblical scholarship and experiential modes of teaching the Scriptures. In distinctive ways, Walter, Hans Reudi Weber, and Conrad L'Heureux have each helped me see how the biblical traditions can be related more directly to human experience.

The stream from which lots of folks are swimming into the pool is the Network of Biblical Storytellers and the many persons who have told these stories in ministry in the aftermath of storytelling festivals, courses, and workshops. This network of fellow storytellers is the source of many elements in this book: stories about telling biblical stories, educational processes, and the book's overall spirit of good cheer. In particular, Margaret Eddy, Mal Bertram, Judy Gorsuch, Ken

Parker, Richard Rice, Paul Neff, and Louise Mahan have contributed stories and materials to this book. The spirit of Clay Woodbury, Pam Moffatt, Gary Vencill, and the many members of the Network of Biblical Storytellers is evident throughout this book.

A beautiful quiet stream which led to this book is the stream of the Spirit to which I was guided by my spiritual directors: Margo Merz; Michael Cooper, S.J.; and Richard Bollman, S.J. They, along with the community of the Jesuit Renewal Center, have generously shared the gifts of prayer and Ignatian spirituality with me. The ways of seeing and listening to God that I have learned through their spiritual companionship have made it possible for me to find this lovely pool through what appeared to be impenetrable thickets. This book has been formed by a unique confluence of Roman Catholic and Protestant traditions.

Another stream that has fed this pool is Abingdon Press. Ron Patterson has persisted in this project, and Robert Conn is the kind of editor every book should have, namely, someone who genuinely loves the topic. I cannot imagine a happier convergence of streams of energy than has happened with Bob and the Press in this project.

The communities of theological education where I have been privileged to teach have provided the ground on which this pool has been formed. New York Theological Seminary and its commitment to contextual, professional education literally drove me to make biblical scholarship directly relate to the practice of ministry. And my colleagues there, in particular Melvin Schoonover, Willis Elliott, Bob Washington, William Weisenbach, and George W. Webber, supported and encouraged me. At United Theological Seminary, I have received warm administrative support and the gift of time from Newell Wert and Leonard Sweet, which has helped to make this work possible. My colleagues on the faculty, in particular Irvin Batdorf, James Nelson, and Tyron Inbody, have given significant help. Dennis Benson provided camaraderie and the wisdom of his experience during the process of writing the manuscript. Ann DeHays has contributed patience, skill, and good cheer in the various stages of the manuscript's preparation. And the staff of the library, led by Elmer O'Brien, has been a model of support in the years of this project's evolution.

Finally, there is my family. When Tom, now twenty-one, was not yet a year old, he was crawling around under the typewriter as I began the search that led eventually to this pool. Both Michael and Tom have been my most sympathetic and responsive listeners over the years. They have no idea how much I have learned from them about the meaning of the stories. Jean has walked beside me throughout this quest. Without her love and support, the search would have ended in the slough of despond.

Several persons dove into this manuscript and made suggestions that have made it far more accessible and clear: David Rhoads, Margo Merz, Pam Moffatt, Ken Kreuger, Gary Vencill, Gil Bartholomew, Pat Linnemann, and Dennis Benson. Bob Peiffer, Bruce Hartley, and Addie Clark have given valuable help at various stages of this work.

That is the general description of the pool and its most present springs and streams. But, as with all woodland pools, it is only clear and living rather than stagnant because rivers and streams flow out from the pool and water the ground all around. Only the continued sharing of the stories will make it possible for the tradition to live. You are invited, therefore, to tiptoe, walk slowly, jump, or dive head first into the world of the gospel as storytelling and to join a wonderful group of people who love to tell the stories of God's presence and action in Jesus Christ.

STORY
JOURNEY

BEGINNINGS

Let me tell you a story about a story journey. During a retreat at the Jesuit Renewal Center in Cincinnati, I went down to the Little Miami River, which runs past the center. It was a wonderfully warm sixth of March. I decided to hike up the riverbank. It looked easy enough. A broad area of sand and rocks lay ahead. But around the first bend, there was a steep bank covered with brambles. It looked overwhelming; and for me, frightening and risky. I remember saying to myself: "My knees are wrecked from the accident. (I was hit by a car thirteen years ago.) This is an isolated spot. If I fell, I might really get hurt and not be found for a day or so." It was discouraging and I almost quit.

I stood there looking at this embankment, the latest in a long series of insuperable obstacles in my life. Because I had been steadily praying, I asked something like, "What is there in this that you want me to know?" And my memories went back to the people of Israel in the wilderness of Sinai, to Elijah on his journey to the mountain, and to Jesus in the wilderness of Judea. The memory of those stories gave me a new perspective from which to look at this obstacle. Instead of being overwhelming, the bank looked more like an adventure, an invitation to a kind of pilgrimage. The memory steadied me. After several minutes I saw a possible path, some roots for handholds, and slowly, I clambered up and over!

It was exhilarating! And it was the beginning of a journey almost two miles up the river and back. It was by far the longest hike I had taken in the thirteen years since the accident. And at a number of places along the way, the same thing happened. At another steep bank, I was suddenly afraid. This time the story of David and Goliath flashed into my mind, and the memories of David gave me courage. At another place I had to inch my way down a bank and across a trunk that lay over a four-foot section of rushing water. This time I remembered Jesus walking on the water and Peter walking to him on the water. The trunk looked pretty insignificant in that context.

As I walked back along a bank high above the river, I could see my whole life's journey before me. It was connected with other journeys: Israel, Jesus, my faith community, my family. Our lives are story journeys. The events of our lives connect with many other stories. But at the deepest and most profound level, the stories of our lives are empowered and given meaning by being connected with God's story. I was overwhelmed with gratitude at the gift of the stories of the Scriptures. They had literally enabled me to make this journey.

At that moment, the idea for this book occurred to me. The idea was to offer the stories as a gift to anyone who faces obstacles and embankments in their way. This book is an invitation to a story journey, to learn the stories of the Gospels as a resource for your life journey.

The gospel was originally a storytelling tradition. This storytelling character of the gospel is reflected in the history of the word. "Gospel" is a shortened form of an Old English word, "godspell." It means: "god" = good, "spell" = tale— "good tale." The original definition of "spell" also reflects this storytelling character of the "godspell." A spell was a spoken word or set of words believed to have magic power. In Old English, therefore, the word that was the best equivalent for the Latin word, *evangelium*, was a tale whose telling had power.

This Latin word, *evangelium*, was in turn a transliteration of the Greek *euangelion.* This word also had two parts, *eu,* meaning "good," and *angelion,* which was related to "angel," a messenger. It meant "good news." The word *euangelion* could refer to both the message and the messenger. Thus in Greek tradition a *euangelion* could also be a messenger who delivered the good news of victories in battle.

Only later did the gospel become associated with books. In the liturgical tradition of the Church, the gospel has been the weekly reading from the Gospels. The association with the book has often been symbolized by the elevation of or procession with the Gospel book as a part of this reading during worship. Still later, the gospel has come to refer to a set of ideas that are a summation of the basic beliefs of the Christian religion. In fact, the Church now tends to think of the gospel as a set of abstract ideas based on the study of the canonical documents but divorced from story. The gospel has lost its original character as a living storytelling tradition of messengers who told the good news of the victory of Jesus.

The purpose of this book is to recover the gospel as storytelling. The problem is that telling biblical stories is foreign to contemporary experience. We continue to read Bible stories to children. But the assumption is that once you grow up and learn to think, you will stop telling stories and start telling the truth. Telling the truth means that you will speak in conceptual abstractions.

The only way to start an exploration of the gospel as storytelling is to learn to tell the stories. Until you have experienced the stories as stories, all arguments about the meaningfulness of "telling" the stories will be more or less meaningless abstractions. This book is, therefore, a guide to a journey into the gospel tradition in its original medium, oral narrative. It does not provide an overall theory or relate the topic to the movements in biblical exegesis and theology out of which it grows. It includes suggestions about how the gospel as storytelling can be a resource for ministry: in preaching and worship, pastoral care, Christian education, social action, and prayer. And there is an extensive bibliography that can provide resources for further exploration. But the assumption of this book is that *no one,* not even the most learned scholar, can understand the gospel as storytelling without first learning to tell the stories.

This book is organized as a gradual introduction to the processes of biblical storytelling through learning and telling a series of stories from the Gospels. It is a guide for women and men who want to enter more deeply into a relationship with Jesus' journey from his birth, through the events of his ministry of teaching and healing, to the victory of his passion, death, and resurrection. To enter into this tradition is to begin a story journey.

But why story and why storytelling? Story is a primary language of experience. Telling and listening to a story has the same structure as our experience. To paraphrase Stephen Crites, experience has a narrative quality. The episodes of our lives take place one after another just like a story. One of the ways we know each other is by telling our stories. We live in stories.

And storytelling is the primal medium of story. I remember reading an advertisement for a novel by William Faulkner. "The greatest American storyteller of our time," the ad said. I knew about Faulkner as a person from my studies as an English major. He was a shy person, a man of few words, who rarely told stories. Faulkner wrote some of the greatest novels of this century. But he didn't tell many stories. He wrote books that were intended to be read by persons who would sit in an armchair and read in silence.

Telling a story to another person or to a group, face to face, is different from reading a book. It has its own unique dynamics. Storytelling is fun, engaging, spontaneous, and playful. To say "Let me tell you a story" is like saying "Let's go play." Everyone loves a good story.

Storytelling creates community. Persons who tell each other stories become friends. And men and women who know the same stories deeply are bound together in special ways. Furthermore, good stories get retold and form an ever-expanding storytelling network. There is something about a good story that virtually demands retelling. New connections are established between persons who have heard and identified with the same stories. And the deeper the meaning of the story, the deeper are the relationships that are formed by the sharing.

Storytelling is also highly emotional. To laugh and to cry, to be deeply moved and to get so involved that you have to know how the story came out in the end—that is storytelling. You get to know other people and you get to know yourself. And the stories you remember and tell to others become the best gifts you have to give. They become yours in a special way. People become the stories they love to tell.

And why the stories of the Gospels? There are lots of stories in the world. Every human community has its stories. But the stories of the Bible have a special meaning that makes them distinctive. The stories of Israel—the patriarchs and matriarchs of Genesis, Moses and the Exodus, the judges such as Deborah and Gideon, the kings David and Saul, and the prophets Elijah, Isaiah, Jeremiah, Daniel—have formed a unique storytelling tradition. In these stories, the people of Israel throughout the ages have experienced the actions and presence of God. These stories have been remembered as the stories of the God of Israel. By remembering and telling them, Israel experiences those events again. God becomes present and active in the storytelling event. Retelling these particular stories has enabled the physical and spiritual descendants of Abraham and Sarah to know God.

The stories of Jesus of Nazareth were formed by persons who were a part of Israel's storytelling tradition. The stories of Jesus, both those by him and those about him, were told by his followers as the fulfillment of Israel's hope for a Messiah. They were also stories that uniquely revealed the very character of God. The stories of Jesus' birth, his ministry of healing and reconciliation, his teachings, and his death and resurrection became for them stories about the decisive and central action of God in all of human history. In telling and listening to the stories of Jesus, early Christians made connections with their own lives that made clear to them how God was present. And the uniquely revelatory character of these stories has been confirmed in the experience of millions of people over the ages.

The witness of these men and women of faith is that these stories are somehow distinctively true.

When the stories were recorded in the Gospels, they were written down so that they could be read aloud and relearned. By writing them, the evangelists preserved their original forms so that they could be reheard and retold. To learn and tell the stories to ourselves and to others is to go back to the source. It is a return to the spring from which the early church drank. This is the root meaning of "authority." The heart of the word is "author." The authority of the Scriptures is based on their role as the source of our knowledge of God. Thus, entering into the story journey of the gospel tradition is a pilgrimage to a primary source of the revelation of God in Jesus Christ.

The surprises of this story journey are the constant intersections. The route of a journey consists of a series of intersections where roads come together. The experience of the story journey is surprising because of the ways that the Jesus stories intersect with others and shed new light on them. Three kinds of intersections come to mind: my story, our story, and Jesus' story.

Thus, the events of my trip up the river were enlightened by the connections that emerged with the stories of Israel and Jesus. There was an entirely different meaning to that walk because of the biblical stories with which it was associated. But the enlightenment was reciprocal. The biblical stories were also given new meaning by being connected with my experience. And in turn both my story and the biblical stories are given new meaning by their intersection with the stories of other persons who face obstacles as a result of the accidents of history.

The same is true of the stories of our various communities. Every community—family, local congregation, town and city, nation and denomination—has its own stories. When these communal narratives are connected with God's story in a deep and appropriate manner, authentic revelation takes place.

The mark of authentic revelation is an appropriate connection to the sacred story. This is the reason historical study of the Gospel narratives is an essential aspect of the story journey. In the absence of historical study, the connections that people make with the stories are sometimes inappropriate. The most typical problem is reading our experience back into the story in ways that are incongruent with the biblical story. Appropriate connections grow out of experiencing the meaning of the story in its original historical context. To be authentic, the connection must mutually relate to the meaning and life context of both. The story journey requires, therefore, that we listen closely to these ancient tales.

But when our/my story is connected appropriately with the story of God, there is revelation. It is a sacramental moment when ordinary human reality discloses the presence of God. Through the words of the story, the Word of God becomes present. In that moment, it becomes a sacred story through which God speaks.

Through the stories, Jesus Christ becomes present. There is a sense in which Jesus tells his own story, first to and through the evangelists and then to and through us. And when these moments of authentic connection take place, Jesus is really there. Thus, telling the stories of the Gospels is one of the forms of the real presence of Christ.

If you want to take this kind of journey, you are invited to come along. None of us knows where the journey will ultimately lead. But this story journey will be a resource for the life of the Spirit and for the ministry of the community of faith. As your guide, I promise that. It will be a source of renewal and new life.

1

BIRTH

(Luke 2:1-20)

In Luke, the beginning of Jesus' journey is the story of his
birth. It is an appropriate place to begin our journey into the
gospel. Luke's birth narrative is probably told more frequently
than any other story. During the Christmas season, it is read in
local churches and homes, performed in pageants, and recited
on television. It has become a romanticized narrative, full of
sentimentality. But rarely is it told in a manner that is
appropriate to its original meaning and intent.

The first step in the journey is to get the story off the page or
out of the air and inside yourself. The goal is to master the story
so that it can be told without fear. Learning to tell a story is a
natural process. We do it virtually every day in some form. We
hear stories of various kinds and retell them regularly.
Retelling stories we have heard from someone else is the stuff
of rumors, jokes, and mealtimes. Learning to tell biblical
stories is an extension of the same process.

There are many different ways of learning and remembering
stories. In the end, we each develop our own distinctive
processes. But identifying some basic principles can be helpful
for a successful beginning. I will give some hints that have
worked for others. From that start, you can build your own
system.

Learning the Story

The most natural way to learn a story is by hearing it told well and then retelling it. That is the way in which stories are learned in oral cultures. But most people who learn biblical stories in literate cultures do it alone, working with a text. Thus, while I recommend that you listen to the telling of the stories whenever possible and that you find a partner and learn a story together, this first set of suggestions assumes that you will often be working by yourself.

Listening for the Structure

The first principle of learning a story is to identify the structure of the story. Once the structure is clearly in mind, the words can be hung on that mental frame.

A biblical story is a series of sounds. The beginnings and endings of the sounds are marked by breaths. A sentence is usually the sounds that can be spoken in one breath. The sentences or breath units are grouped in episodes. An episode is a story unit of two to four sentences. The sentences and episodes are the foundational components of a biblical story's structure.

In the text that follows, Luke's birth narrative is arranged in sentences and episodes. I suggest that you read the story aloud and listen for its structure. A period and a new sentence at the margin is the sign for a breath. The end of an episode is indicated by a row of stars and stands for a longer pause. In storytelling, taking time for a relaxed, deep breath between episodes is always appropriate.

This text is the Revised Standard Version translation, with only slight modifications. I have chosen this text because it is the most widely used translation tradition in contemporary English-speaking churches. However, if you prefer or are already familiar with another translation, learn that one. All translations of the Gospel stories from the original Greek are approximations of the originals. And different translations have different values. At a number of points along the way, I will include adaptations which modify the Revised Standard Version for storytelling, as well as original translations of my own that render the repetitions and connotations of the Greek more accurately. The goal is to hear and to tell the story as fully and clearly as possible.

The Story

In those days a decree went out from Caesar Augustus that all the world should be enrolled.

This was the first enrollment, when Quirinius was governor of Syria.

And all went to be enrolled, each to his own city.

☆ ☆ ☆ ☆ ☆

And Joseph also went up from Galilee, from the city of Nazareth, to Judea, to the city of David, which is called Bethlehem, because he was of the house and lineage of David, to be enrolled with Mary, his betrothed, who was with child.

And while they were there, the time came for her to be delivered and she gave birth to her first-born son.

And she wrapped him in swaddling cloths, and laid him in a manger, because there was no place for them in the inn.

☆ ☆ ☆ ☆ ☆

And in that region there were shepherds out in the field, keeping watch over their flock by night.

And an angel of the Lord appeared to them, and the glory of the Lord shone around them.

And they were filled with fear.

☆ ☆ ☆ ☆ ☆

And the angel said to them, "Be not afraid; for behold, I bring you good news of a great joy which will come to all the people, for to you is born this day in the city of David a Savior, who is Christ the Lord.

And this will be a sign for you: you will find a babe
wrapped in swaddling cloths and lying in a manger."
And suddenly there was with the angel a multitude of the
heavenly host praising God and saying, "Glory to
God in the highest, and on earth peace among men
with whom he is pleased."

☆　☆　☆　☆　☆

When the angels went away from them into heaven, the
shepherds said to one another, "Let us go over to
Bethlehem and see this thing that has happened,
which the Lord has made known to us."
And they went with haste, and found Mary and Joseph,
and the babe lying in a manger.
And when they saw it they made known the saying which
had been told them concerning this child.

☆　☆　☆　☆　☆

And all who heard it wondered at what the shepherds told
them.
But Mary kept all these things, pondering them in her heart.
And the shepherds returned, glorifying and praising God
for all they had heard and seen, as it had been told
them.

Having read the story aloud, you can now identify some of
the characteristics of oral narratives.

Variations in tempo. In order to read in one or even two
breaths the sentences about the trip from Nazareth up to
Bethlehem (vss. 4-5) and the angel's first words to the
shepherds (vss. 10-11), it is necessary to read rapidly. The short
sentences—"And they were filled with fear," "And all went to
be enrolled," "But Mary kept all these things"— can be read
more slowly. This more leisurely pace gives the listener more
time to think over what these words might mean.

Emphasis. The contrast in tempo between different sentences creates emphasis. For example, two of the short
sentences conclude an episode (vss. 3, 9b). Since episode

endings are accentuated by the longer pause between the episodes, the content of those sentences naturally receives more emphasis. The pause gives the listeners more time to reflect on these final words. This end position, combined with the slower pace of a short sentence, makes these two sentences more emphatic. In Luke's story, this concluding emphasis is given to the description of the enrollment and the shepherds' fear. This principle of "end emphasis" is present throughout the biblical storytelling tradition. In this story, it is easy to hear how it works.

Verbal threads. The episodes of the story are tied together by linked sounds. Verbal threads are words that are repeated either exactly or with minor variations. The verbal thread that ties the whole story together is "wrapped him in swaddling cloths, laid [lying] him in a manger" (vss. 7, 12, 16). The story's beginning is connected by the verbal thread "enrollment" (enrolled), which occurs in each of the first four sentences of the story (vss. 1-5). Verbal threads in the story's midsection are "the city of David" (vss. 5, 11) and "praising God" (vss. 13, 20). The conclusion is knit together by variations on the theme of the shepherds' hearing and retelling what the angel told them: ". . . made known the saying which *had been told them,"* ". . . wondered at what the shepherds *told them,"* ". . . as it *had been told them"* (vss. 17-18, 20). I find it no coincidence that the confirmation of the truth of the story is connected with the hearing and telling of stories.

Naming and Picturing the Structure

The episodes are chunks of the story that are unified by a theme or an image. A step in learning the story is to identify each episode with a name. My names for these episodes are the enrollment, the birth, the shepherds, the announcement, the confirmation, and the responses. These themes or subjects also help to recall the key words of each episode.

The story is then learned episode by episode. When I am learning a new story by myself, I often create a rough chart of the key words in each episode. The most important words are the episode's beginning and ending. In between are the key words at the core of the story. My chart of the first episode might look something like this:

In those days   decree   Caesar Augustus   enrolled.

first enrollment   Quirinius, governor of Syria.

Everyone   enrolled   each   own city.

In effect, these words become names for the chunks in which I learn the story. The key words are the story's verbal skeleton.

Equally important are the images of the story. For people who are visually oriented, images are the very stuff of memory. Luke's narrative is unusually vivid in its images: the emperor and the governor issuing their decrees, the journey up to Bethlehem and the birth in a stable, the shepherds with their flocks, the angel and the angel choir, the shepherds and the family in the stable. These images are so striking that they are hard to forget.

Episode beginnings are the first place to look for images. That is usually where you will find both settings in time and place and introductions of new characters. In this story, the scene shifts from the palace of Caesar Augustus to Bethlehem to the shepherds' fields outside the town and then back to the birthplace in Bethlehem. Identifying an image for each episode fixes the episode in the mind as a unified whole or gestalt.

Luke's word pictures have the same style as Japanese paintings. In a minimalist manner, he draws a strong line here and a vivid color there. He outlines a verbal image that the listeners can fill out in their imaginations. If a storyteller sees the image vividly, the story will be remembered more easily.

Some people have found that creating visual images of a story, in either symbols or cartoons, helps them remember it. Picture writing worked for the Egyptians and, in a different style, the Chinese. It might work for you.

Thinking the Story

Many people start trying to memorize a story by repeating the words over and over. This learning strategy is most effective when the story is rethought rather than more or less mindlessly regurgitated. One way of thinking the story is to group the words into chunks that are as large as possible. Just as "supercalifragilisticexpialidotious" is one word, so also is "inthosedaysadecreewentoutfromCaesarAugustus." As the story is repeated, these chunks of words are hung on the structure of the names, key words, and images that have been identified and learned. Remembering the story is then a process of rethinking these word chunks. Once you have identified the structure of verbal and pictorial thoughts and internalized them, the words are simply present in memory as the means for thinking those thoughts.

Learning stories is best done in the dead spaces of time: before and after bedtime, riding in the car, taking a shower or working on the face in front of the mirror with a razor or makeup, waiting for an appointment. My good friend David Rhoads, with whom I usually room at scholarly meetings, is invariably reciting some story or another in the shower. By learning a little bit day by day, he has learned, among others, the Gospel of Mark, the Revelation to John, and Galatians.

Memory research has also discovered that the best pattern for repetition is short and frequent repetitions with progressively longer intervals in between. A pattern for the repetition of a short story might be: first day—four times during the day and twice more before bedtime; second day—twice in the shower and three times during an hour of the day; third day—once in the morning and two times during the day; fifth day—once in the morning or at bedtime. In order to keep the stories in the memory, they need to be repeated. Finding occasions when you can tell the stories is essential for keeping the memory fresh. That's why storytellers go around looking for people who will listen. Retelling the stories is the only way to keep them.

There is no substitute for repetition. But repetition primarily retains data in short-term memory. The key to storing a story in long-term memory is to associate the words with episodic and semantic structures of sounds, images, and gestures. By working out your own recipe of memory processes, the story will be yours to enjoy and to share with others.

Word for Word or in My Own Words?

Before reading any further, I would suggest that you learn the first two episodes of Luke's narrative. And the first question always is, should I learn the story word for word or can I learn it in my own words? Learning biblical stories raises a distinctive set of issues for storytellers because the text of the story is often so well known. It is like telling the story of the three little pigs to a four-year-old who has heard it fifty times. If you change the words of the big bad wolf, you'll quickly be told that you got it wrong.

Furthermore, the authors of the Gospels were skilled storytellers who knew what they were doing. For example, the first thing that beginning storytellers tend to do is to add lots of words. The assumption is that these were primitive authors and that we are now more sophisticated. Since every extra word slows down the story's action, the effect is to make the story longer and more boring. Biblical storytellers learned from experience how easily a listener can lose interest. For this reason, they spent words like misers. These stories were perfected by decades of retelling. Like a rolling stone, the rough edges of the story were worn off until it was smooth and shiny.

The stories of the Bible are probably the most powerful narratives in the history of world literature. We honor Shakespeare and other poets by learning their poems word for word. We perform the music of Mozart, Bach, and Beethoven with minute precision. Why not honor biblical storytellers with the respect that they deserve?

However, in most churches, the actual words that were written by the biblical authors in Hebrew, Aramaic, and Greek are neither read nor learned. The Hebrew text of the Bible continues to be recited and memorized in synagogues. But in Western churches, vernacular translations are read rather than the original Hebrew and Greek. Furthermore, as is evident in the variations of the same stories in the Gospels themselves, storytelling invites some degree of improvisation. The rote recitation of exactly the same words in every telling can become deadly. Therefore, a preoccupation with getting every word of an English translation exactly right is probably inappropriate.

Nevertheless, as Alec McGowen has shown, the recitation of the exact words of a first-rate translation can be a powerful form of biblical storytelling.

The best approach is to treat biblical stories like a jazz pianist treats a classic tune. A jazz pianist will first learn the music in its original form. Then he can improvise on it. Many of the world's great organists improvise a postlude on the tune of the final hymn. On the other side of mastery, good improvisation is possible. Sometimes, as in some settings of public worship, it is appropriate to tell biblical stories word for word exactly as they are received. On more informal occasions or in a sermon, various degrees of improvisational retelling are wonderful.

I would suggest, therefore, that you first learn the story as close to word for word as possible. An initial goal might be 75 percent verbal accuracy. As you work with the story, you will grow into it more deeply and it will be easier to remember. Having mastered the story in its original form, you will then be able to improvise on it appropriately and with confidence.

As soon as possible after you have learned it, tell it to someone. I find that if I tell a joke within a few hours after I've heard it, I will remember it. But if I wait until the next day, it is gone. If no one is available, tell it into a tape recorder or to a friend with whom you can talk in your imagination. When my son Michael was young he had an imaginary friend, Joe Nagry from Mr. Roger's neighborhood, to whom he told wonderful stories for many months. Good friends make good story-listeners, even if they are present only in memory or imagination.

Listening to the Story

Biblical storytelling is like an archaeological dig. We are seeking to hear an ancient story so that we can retell it appropriately. A biblical text records the story's sounds. And as you become sensitive to the patterns of the stories, you can discern the clues to the sounds. How then did Luke's story sound when it was originally told?

Background

The enrollment. The storytellers who formed the stories of Luke's Gospel lived in the aftermath of the Jewish war. The war took place between A.D. 66–70. It was begun by Jewish Zealots who believed that true faith meant giving allegiance to the God of Israel *alone*. Any signs of allegiance to emperors or kings were anathema and were considered apostasy. This included paying Roman taxes. The story of the Pharisees questioning Jesus about paying taxes to Caesar reflects this issue (Matt. 22:15-22; Mark 12:13-17; Luke 20:20-26).

The Zealots stood in the tradition of the Maccabees. In 167 B.C., Mattathias, a rural priest and the father of five sons, killed a Jew who was going to offer a sacrifice at an altar to Zeus (I Macc. 2). These altars and mandatory sacrifices were part of a campaign by Antiochus Epiphanes, the Syrian king, to abolish the Jewish law and establish Hellenistic religion and culture in Israel. Jews who cooperated with the Syrians were considered traitors by zealous Jews like Mattathias.

This tradition of Jewish rebellion against Hellenistic rulers was a response to centuries of political oppression. With the exception of the brief period of Jewish independence from 142–63 B.C., which resulted from the Maccabean revolt, the people of Israel were ruled by various Gentile emperors from 587 B.C. on: Babylonians (587–539 B.C.), Persians (539–332 B.C.), Hellenists (332–142 B.C.), and Romans (since 63 B.C.).

This history is the background for Luke's story. Luke sets Jesus' birth in the context of the enrollment ordered by Caesar Augustus at the time of Quirinius. As far as we know from ancient historical sources, the only such enrollment in Palestine took place in A.D. 6 (Reicke 1968, 135-36). Its purpose was tax collection. The first Zealot revolt took place at this time. Under the leadership of Judas the Galilean and Zadok, a Pharisee, an attempt was made to sabotage the enrollment. The extent of the revolt is unclear and may often be overestimated (Rhoads, 1976, 47-52). Despite the resistance, whatever its extent, Quirinius succeeded in carrying out the enrollment. The enrollment was probably remembered in the period of the Lukan storytellers as a time of conflict over Roman rule. It was only the latest in a long series of oppressive actions by Gentile emperors. The enrollment under Quirinius was told and heard, therefore, in the context of this history.

The first chapter of Luke's Gospel describes the miraculous conception and birth of John the Baptist and Mary's conversations with the angel Gabriel and her kinswoman Elizabeth. These are the immediate contexts for the birth narrative in Luke 2. I would suggest that you read them aloud along with a good commentary (e.g., Raymond Brown, *The Birth of the Messiah*).

Details of the Story

David. Luke associates Jesus' birth with David, during whose reign Israel experienced its greatest power. The long sentence describing the trip up to Bethlehem includes verbal threads which recall the memories of David: "to the city of David which is called Bethlehem, because he was of the house and lineage of David" (vs. 4). It is extremely rare in biblical narrative for a name to be repeated twice in the same sentence. But Luke repeats David's name twice so that Jesus' relationship to him cannot be missed.

Mary. Because an intense identification with Mary has been evoked in the earlier stories of her encounters with Gabriel and Elizabeth, this brief description—"Mary, his betrothed, who was with child"—calls back all of those associations (vs. 4). Having heard the stories of Gabriel's visit to Mary and of her ecstatic conversation with Elizabeth (Luke 1:39-56), Luke's listeners knew it was probable that Mary would become pregnant. But these words both confirm the prophecy and set it in a new context. The story invites the listener who has identified with Mary to think back over this long trip up to Joseph's hometown from her point of view. The tone of the words is tender.

"Gave birth to her first-born son." The punctuation of the sentence determines whether this phrase is part of the second or third sentence in the episode (vs. 7). It seems to me that the birth is the climax of the second part of the episode. The sentence describes the inconvenient and embarrassing context of the birth and ends with the birth itself. The final sentence is then more intimate and focuses on Mary's care for her newborn son in difficult circumstances.

The shepherds' fear. The phrase describing the shepherds' fear is highly emphatic; literally translated, it says, "And the shepherds feared a great fear" (vs. 9). Luke was seeking to evoke ultimate fear.

The translation of the last phrase of the angels' song is problematic (vs. 14). "Men" here is used as a generic term but is often heard now as sex-specific. Furthermore, most grammarians conclude that *eudokias* refers to humanity as the object rather than the subject of God's good pleasure. Thus, rather than "with whom he is pleased," a better translation is "on whom his pleasure rests." Therefore, the most accurate translation now would be "to all people on whom God's pleasure rests."

The final episode reports the responses of, first, the people who heard about the sign, then Mary, and, finally, the shepherds (vss. 18-20). Each of these descriptions is an insight into their internal perceptions and responses. These inside views increase the sympathetic characteristics of these characters at the climax of the story.

Comments on the Individual Episodes

The enrollment. The major question in telling this episode is the storyteller's attitude toward the enrollment. My conclusion is that the narrator's attitude was not positive. The usual sentimental tone for reading this story, which presents Caesar Augustus and Quirinius with the same nostalgia and warmth as Santa Claus, is thoroughly inappropriate. Resignation, cynicism, or hostility are all possible attitudes for an appropriate retelling. Luke is describing political and economic oppression by an alien dictatorship. The decree's effect was to require everyone to travel to their hometowns and register for a census that enabled the Romans to collect taxes more efficiently. The effect of the episode for Luke's listeners was to recall that time of political oppression which sowed the seeds for the Jewish war.

The journey. This long sentence (vss. 4-5) does not have to be told with the speed that is required to do it in one breath. It may instead have the kind of trudging tempo of a long journey. Such a tempo emphasizes its heaviness. It is relieved by the memories of David. Furthermore, the journey's poignancy is heightened by the implied tenderness in the relationship between Joseph and his pregnant fiancée, Mary, at the end. The phrase "while they were there" calls attention to the inconvenience and stress of Mary's being away from home at the time of this birth (vs. 6).

The ethical norms shared by Luke and his listeners also shaped the meaning of this episode. In Jewish culture, it was irregular for a couple to have a child before they were married. Furthermore, this birth took place in Joseph's ancestral hometown. Disapproval and ostracism may be implied in the failure of Joseph's family to extend hospitality to Joseph and Mary. If so, this implied disapproval of the people of Bethlehem is later transformed into their wonder at what the shepherds told them. An opposite reversal takes place in the subsequent story of Jesus' first sermon in Nazareth (Luke 4:16-30). The people are at first pleased, but their response is transformed into violent offense.

The shepherds. The rest of the story is experienced primarily from the perspective of the shepherds. The initial identification with the shepherds is established in the introductory episode (vss. 8-9) by a relatively long inside view. The narrator describes the shepherds watching their flock, the appearance of the angel, and their internal feelings of fear. The effect is to see and hear the event from the shepherds' point of view. The shepherds are relatively "low-life" characters, not unlike Falstaff and his cronies in Shakespeare's plays. A little bit of that folksiness in the telling is thoroughly appropriate.

The announcement. Angels have a problem in biblical stories. They have to get persons to calm down before they can deliver their messages. The style of this angel may be more "cool" and relaxed than the usual heavy and authoritative manner of traditional readings. Angels were, after all, mediators between humans and God. The angel in Luke has a distinctive character that needs to be caught appropriately. The angel's announcement is followed by the identification of a sign that will confirm the good news (vss. 11-12). This may be in response to the implicit disbelief of the shepherds.

The climax of the episode is the song of the angel choir, which is appropriately sung in a broad and celebrative manner (vss. 13-14). The melody is less important than the mood.

The confirmation. An image in my mind for the shepherds' response is Abbott and Costello after they have seen a ghost. It is a combination of excitement and relief. An appropriate improvisation at the beginning for me is "Hey, you guys, let's . . ." (vs. 15). The narrator's report of the discovery of the family expresses the shepherds' wonder and amazement at what they were seeing, rather than being a mere description (vss. 16-17). And the description of their report needs to be told in the spirit in which they told it to Mary and Joseph.

The responses. Each of these responses has a distinctive spirit: first, the amazement of everyone who heard, then the meditative pondering of Mary, and, finally, the joy of the shepherds (vss. 18-20). Mary's quiet response is surrounded by the enthusiasm of the people and the shepherds.

Connections

One of the gifts of a storyteller is to bring the distinctiveness of her or his experience to the telling of the story. If people do this, hearing the same biblical stories retold over and over again is never boring, because the story is always different. Each person gives the story a distinctive nuance and shape. The same words can have radically different meanings when told by different people. This distinctiveness emerges naturally as the story is internalized. Throughout this book, I will make some suggestions about fields of personal and communal experience that you might explore. Connecting our experiences of life with biblical stories gives our telling of the stories depth and distinctiveness.

Personal experiences. The episode of Jesus' birth connects most directly with the memories and experiences of childbirth. Mothers, fathers, and siblings all have different contributions to make to the telling of these stories. One way of exploring these connections is to think about and retell the stories of the births you remember. In remembering and retelling those stories, especially with the others who were involved, the special quality of birth stories shines forth. It is also fun to ask parents and grandparents to tell the stories they remember about your birth.

The angel's announcement to the shepherds is also connected with another type of experience, the experience of telling someone good news. The most important associations with the spirit of this story are these experiences of delivering good news. Announcements of births, weddings, awards, victories, good health; opening letters with good news in them—these are all instances. These experiences have in common that unique delight of knowing something that will make the other person happy, and, if you see in their eyes that they don't believe it, having the evidence to prove it. You might make a list now of those times when you have had good news to tell. The full range is appropriate, from little daily victories to the big ones.

For example, I remember the moments of telling my sister that I was going to get married, calling my folks when our sons were born, and announcing to my wife that I had successfully passed my doctoral exam. Once again, I would suggest that you tell some of those stories and listen to others tell them to you. In that process, you will catch the unique spirit of the announcements of the angel and the shepherds.

When Luke's story is told, let the connections you have discovered be expressed. Generally, our tellings of biblical stories are disassociated from human experience. The vitality and enthusiasm that comes from letting these connections emerge is appropriate to the stories. But equally important is that the stories of the actions of God also shed new light and spirit on our stories.

Communal experiences. The communal context of the story of Jesus' birth is the experience of political and economic oppression. Jesus was born in a manger in Bethlehem because his parents had to register to pay taxes to a foreign dictatorship. Connecting with experiences of political and economic oppression now is, therefore, also a resource for hearing and telling this story well. What experiences of oppression have you and those with whom you are identified endured? Remembering those stories is one way of exploring the connections of the story of Jesus' birth with your experience.

I will suggest a storytelling process that you might try. Gather together representatives of a community with which you have shared such experiences: fellow students, members of the family, other women or men, other persons who share your work role, other members of your race or nation. Recall your story and some of the things that you have endured and are enduring together. And then tell the story of Jesus' birth.

Later, find and read the story of some group other than your own that has been oppressed. Suggestions would be the people of Cambodia and Vietnam, the peasants of Latin America, the European Jewish community during the Nazi era, the Palestinians in the Middle East, the black community of South Africa or the United States, the mentally handicapped, or refugees from southeast Asia or Afghanistan. And once again, listen to Jesus' birth narrative and the ways in which it intersects with their story.

What Luke's narrative will mean I cannot predict or foretell. And people will probably respond in a variety of ways. The stories do not mean only one thing. They are uniquely connected with God and may set our experience of subjection to political and economic powers beyond our control in the context of God's presence in our midst.

Telling the Story

The spirit and style of biblical storytelling is a spirit of sharing. Telling the stories of God is something that everyone can do well. It requires only someone who will live with the story, let it grow in them, and then tell it to another person. And the most basic time for telling these stories is when two or three persons are together.

Stories can be interpreted in many ways. The most important criterion is that the telling should fit the story and the teller. Don't perform or worry about how you are telling it. Having studied and lived with the story, you have prepared enough. Concentrate on the story and on the wonder of Jesus' birth. If you forget, improvise the best you can and just go on. If you remember later in the story, say "Did I tell you that . . . ?" Trust the story.

Telling a biblical story is offering a gift. And there are times when a particular gift is uniquely appropriate. The story of Jesus' birth can be a gift when another person or group feels oppressed or alone. It is usually appropriate to ask whether or not a person would like to hear a story. But if you sense that someone might find the story a gift, offer it to them. They may find it meaningful or they may not. A listener to these stories is free to respond in whatever way he or she chooses, including not at all.

There are also many occasions in which telling this story to a group will be a gift. That requires more practice and care in the telling. The effective telling of a story to a large group is an interpretive art. It has its own challenges and subtleties, as does music or painting. And growth in the art of biblical storytelling is a worthy investment of time and attention. In this story, there are nuances of voice, emotion, inflection, volume, gesture, and pause that may help to make the story live for a group. I would suggest that you tell this story first to children or a small group of friends during the Christmas season. But at any time of the year, many groups will be glad to hear the story of Jesus' birth.

There is a story about the telling of this story that has the surprise and depth of this good news. This account has been written by Paul Neff, an American Baptist pastor, who was at that time working in a small church in Brooklin on the coast of Maine:

I was chaplain for the day at the regional hospital. I noticed that a boy from our town who went to the Pentecostal church was on the patient list. Since it was a regional hospital, we pastors would also visit anyone from our town, regardless of where or whether they went to church. I entered the room of the small boy. It was shortly before Christmas. The little boy was drawing.

"Hello," I said, "my name is Rev. Neff." No response. The little boy keeps drawing.

"I'm the chaplain for the day, and I thought you might like someone to talk to for a bit." No answer. The little boy continues drawing.

"I hear you're a Pentecostal. Do you go to church very often?"

"Sometimes," he said. The little boy goes on drawing.

"Would you like me to tell you a story?"

"Okay." And he kept on drawing.

And so I began to tell him Luke's story of Jesus' birth. I had hardly gotten started when the little boy put down his drawing pencil and began to look at me. About half way through the story, I noticed that tears had begun to roll down his cheeks. When I finished, I asked him, "Why are you crying?"

He said, "It must have been awful lonely for the baby there in the manger."

"It's awful lonely for you here, too, isn't it?" I said. He shook his head and so began our conversation.

2

BAPTISM

(Mark 1:9-13)

In Mark, Jesus' story begins with his baptism. The narrative relates Jesus' inauguration and ordination for his mission in a highly intimate manner. Rather than observing this event from the perspective of a detached observer, the teller of this tale recounts the event from Jesus' point of view, as he sees the dove and hears the voice. As a result, Jesus is introduced as a highly sympathetic person with whom we can identify. He may be a prophet, even the Son of God, but he is one who is already known from the inside out. The storyteller asks us, as listeners, to join Jesus at the beginning of his journey. If we do, his journey becomes our journey. In some sense, we are baptized with Jesus.

Learning the Story

Mark's story was sounds. When persons wrote in the ancient world, they were composing sounds. They assumed that persons who read their writings would read aloud. In turn, the normal practice in the ancient world, particularly with religious traditions, was to memorize that which was read.

One of the reasons stories were memorized had to do with

41

the way ancient scribes wrote. They used no punctuation marks, capitals, or spaces between words. When a scribe reached the end of a line, even if it was in the middle of a word, he moved down to the next line. This is an approximation of how the first episode of Mark's story would have been written. I suggest that you read it out loud and notice the fluidity of your reading:

andithappenedinthosedaysjesuscamefromnazarethin
galileeandwasbaptizedinthejordanbyjohnandimmediate
lyashewascomingupoutofthewaterhesawtheheavenstor
nopenandthespiritasadovecomingdownuponhimanda
voicecameoutoftheheavensyouaremybelovedsonwith
youiamwellpleased

In fact, this manuscript is much easier to read than the ancient manuscripts because the letters are all uniform. You can see why, in order to read the story aloud, it was necessary to memorize it. These texts were not meant for silent reading. Just looking at this one episode gives me a headache!

Because of our reading conventions, we have a primary problem in dealing with biblical narratives. We often assume that the Gospel of Mark, for example, is a text, a series of black marks on pieces of white paper bound together in the middle. But that assumption is false. Those marks on the page are not what Mark composed. Mark's account was never intended to be a soundless text, perceived only with the eyes. Mark's purpose in writing down a story such as Jesus' baptism was to record the sounds in the only available medium.

In fact, during the period in which Mark was written, students in Jewish schools were forbidden to read the sacred literature of Israel in silence. Therefore, if we want to experience Mark's story appropriately, we need to read it aloud and memorize the sounds.

In adapting the Revised Standard Version rendition of this

story, I went back to the Greek text and sought to render into English as many of the repeated and assonant sounds as possible. One reason for doing this is to make it easier to internalize and remember the stories. But it is also because these stories were composed as sounds. Words are repeated and modified with exquisite richness and care. The fullest possible rendering of the sounds of the Greek story in an English translation may help people to hear the story more fully and to learn it more easily.

I would suggest that you find some way of visually connecting the verbal threads in your text with circles and lines, with colors, or with some kind of chart. Then listen for the sound patterns in the story.

The Story

> And it happened in those days Jesus came from Nazareth in Galilee and was baptized in the Jordan by John.
> And immediately as he was coming up out of the water, he saw the heavens torn open and the Spirit, as a dove, coming down upon him.
> And a voice came out of the heavens, "You are my beloved Son; with you I am well pleased."
>
> ☆ ☆ ☆ ☆ ☆
>
> And immediately the Spirit drove him out into the wilderness.
> And he was in the wilderness forty days, tested by Satan.
> And he was with the wild beasts, and the angels served him.

Interiorization

The first step is to get the sounds of Mark's story inside ourselves. I like Walter Ong's name for this process in oral cultures: interiorization. When a story has been learned

43

deeply, it is no longer outside, as an object to be examined. The sounds get inside and resonate, creating vibrations in the interior spaces of the body.

I have found it helpful for story learning to think of myself as having three interior centers: the head, the heart, and the gut or lower belly. Each center has its own kind of associations.

The head stores the words, concepts, and structures of the story. We think the story in our brain space. The heart is the locus of the emotions of the story. The emotional dynamics of a story make us laugh or cry. We feel the story in our hearts. The action of the story happens in the lower belly or bowels. The Greek verb for "to have compassion or pity" names this center best, and you need to say the word in order to sense its meaning: *splagnizomai.* It literally means "to turn over the bowels." In the Gospels, it describes Jesus' feeling of compassion or mercy for someone, such as the leper (Mark 1:41) or the crowd (Matt. 9:36; 14:14). In the bowels, we experience what the story does.

A way of internalizing the story is, therefore, to experience the story with each part of the self and to identify its movements or characteristics. The resonances can then be stored or associated with that moment in the story. Those associations are the stuff of remembering. Just as " to dis-member" means "to cut off parts of the body," "to re-member" means "to embody or flesh out again," to put the parts of the body back together again. To remember is to embody the story's resonance. There the associations can resonate in the interior spaces of the mind, the heart, and the bowels.

Learning the Story with a Partner

These are some suggestions for working with a partner on learning a story. The basic process is to tell it back and forth. Sometimes it helps for one to read it aloud a phrase or sentence at a time and for the other to say it back. Then switch. After both of you have told it two or three times, take two or three minutes to tell it aloud to yourselves. And then tell it to each other. Let me review some elements of the story to notice as you are reciting.

1. Identify the structure of the story. As you are listening or studying, figure out the elements that tie the narrative together. Each chapter of this book begins with the text of a story arranged in episodes. These arrangements of stories are the end result of my critical analysis of the literary units of the gospel narrative. When I am learning a story, I also underline the verbal threads (repeated words) so that they will be easy to identify.

Some groups have found it helpful to make a recording of the story episode by episode and to listen to it. This is fun with a partner, especially if he or she likes to goof off a little. Persons who are visually oriented may make cartoons of stories, a kind of storytelling hieroglyphics. Ron Hill has his wife read him the story, and he says it back to her while drawing cartoons that symbolize the words. Others find it helpful to move with the story and get physically involved in it.

But whether in sound, image, or movement, identifying the structure of the story is an essential step. The more the individual words can be chunked together in blocks, the better.

2. Pay attention to the verbal connections between the episodes of the story. There is a saying about sermons that applies to stories: "Preaching a sermon is like flying an airplane. If you know how to take off and how to get back down on the ground, you can always figure out something in between." The two most important places in a story and in each episode are the beginning and the end. They are your connections. In the pause between the successive episodes, those connections are the life jackets that save the teller of the tale from the abyss of silence and the terror of forgetfulness. And if you pay attention to those life jackets, they are always there. The key is to relax, not panic, and trust that the connections will be there. If your partner is lost, don't jump in right away and save him or her. Relax and remember together.

3. Repeat the story in blocks but never in mindless regurgitation. Always "think" the story rather than merely repeating it. Storytelling is not mere repetition. It is a re-membering of the event. By rethinking the words with the structure and verbal connections in mind, the story will quickly be stored in long-term memory and will never be forgotten.

4. Tell it to your partner from beginning to end. If you forget, just keep going if you can and check out what you missed later. Don't ever stop and say, "I forgot." You didn't forget, you just lost a linkage. Go on with whatever you can remember. After you've gotten to the end, let your partner remind you of the place you forgot.

Tips for Learning the Story

Most of the verbal threads in this story are tied to the story of John the Baptist, which precedes the baptism: baptized, Jordan, John, wilderness. Reading the two stories aloud together is the best way to identify those connections.

But there are also verbal threads within the episodes themselves. In the baptism episode there are "the heavens"—first, torn open, then, a voice—and "out of"—at the beginning of the second and third sentences Jesus comes up "out of" the water and a voice comes "out of" the heavens.

In the testing episode there is a frequent linkage between the last phrase of the first sentence and the first phrase of the next. First he was driven out "into the wilderness," then "he was in the wilderness."

There are also verbal threads tying the two episodes together. "Immediately" precedes both "as he was coming up out of the water" and "the Spirit drove him." This word (*euthus* in Greek) occurs frequently as a linkage throughout Mark and especially in the stories in the first section of the Gospel. The steady repetition of "immediately" gets the narrative off to a fast start. "The Spirit" descends "as a dove" in the first episode and "drove him out" in the second.

By creating these verbal links, the ancient storytellers built in the memory hooks that enabled first themselves and then others to remember and retell their stories.

Images

Each episode begins with a description of the place where it took place: "in the Jordan" and "into the wilderness." By seeing the place in the mind's eye, you can see what happened there: the Jordan, the wilderness, and the wild beasts. Furthermore, the first episode is composed primarily of what Jesus saw and heard: the heavens torn open, the dove, and the voice.

Gestures

It is said that if you tie the hands of storytellers, they can't remember the story. There is truth to this because storytellers remember stories with gestures. Ancient storytellers made vivid and broad gestures that also helped their listeners visualize the story.

In this story, there are many implicit gestures. Coming up out of the water invites a gesture of rising. "He saw the heavens torn open" is appropriately gestured with first a looking up and then a tearing motion. The descent of the dove, the Spirit driving him out, and the angels serving him are elements of the story that are naturally told with gestures as well as words.

Listening to the Story

In Mark's story, the baptism of the crowds by John provides the context of Jesus' baptism. Baptism was an eschatological rite, a once and for all cleansing from sin. It was a sign of purification and repentance in preparation for the new age of the kingdom of God. It stood in contrast to the frequent baths for purification that were characteristic of Israelite religion. As his inauguration, Jesus is baptized in communal solidarity with all those who were being baptized by John. It is a primary sign of his identity with the people of Israel. He does not remain aloof, nor is he, like the kings of Israel, inaugurated by a special rite.

The storyteller immediately moves inside Jesus' mind and relates the rest of the episode from Jesus' point of view. The tearing open of the heavens, the descent of the dove, and the voice are described from Jesus' perspective. Thus, the narrator describes what Jesus saw and heard. The impact of this is to draw the story's listeners into a close relationship with Jesus as a person.

47

Notes on Individual Episodes

The baptism. This is Jesus' ordination for his mission (vs. 9). It is the structural equivalent of the anointings of the kings of Israel (I Sam. 9–10—the anointing of Saul; I Sam. 16—the anointing of David).

The dove. In the story of Noah (Gen. 8:8-12), the dove was the sign of life on the earth and of the end of the long period of darkness in the ark. In Mark's story (vs. 10), the dove is the sign of the Spirit and has all the associations of the end of the age of darkness.

The voice from heaven. Moses, Elijah, and many of the patriarchs and judges of Israel heard a voice from heaven that they knew to be the voice of God. An issue in telling Mark's story is how to speak God's words to Jesus (vs. 11). God's words are usually intoned in a deep, sonorous, and somewhat distant manner. The style is generally that of the unseen big voice in biblical movies and theatrical presentations. It is highly unlikely that this is the manner in which the evangelists told the story. In this saying a loving father first expresses deep affection for his son and then gives him a ringing personal affirmation. This is an intimate word that God says to Jesus himself. We as listeners are permitted to overhear this intimate word.

Driven out into the wilderness. This phrase (vs. 12) calls to mind Israel's forty years of wandering in the wilderness. Not only does this establish a connection between Jesus' experience and that of Israel, but also it makes clear the meaning of this time for Jesus. It was his time of testing. Jesus' tester is, however, different from Israel's. Satan is the symbol of the cosmic powers of evil, the forces of the old age. This episode sets the baptism and Jesus' ministry in the context of the apocalyptic battle between the powers of good and evil.

The wild beasts. Wild beasts were associated with the powers of evil in apocalyptic literature. Thus, the lions in the tale of Daniel in the lions' den (Dan. 6) are a narrative concretization of the beasts in Daniel's apocalyptic visions (Dan. 7–8) who symbolized the powers of evil and the empires of his age. In fact, the words of God to Daniel in these chapters (Dan.

9:22-23; 10:11, 18-19) are a narrative precedent for the more intimate words of God to Jesus.

The angels. Elijah was served food and water by an angel during his forty-day sojourn in the wilderness on his way to Horeb, the mountain of God (I Kings 19:5-8). The presence of the angels here (vs. 13) shows that Jesus, like Elijah, is being tested in a struggle between the powers of good and evil. This in turn makes clear how the story was told. It was not narrated as a simple statement of facts but in a grandiose and apocalyptic manner. Only the style of narration can adequately convey the cosmic character of this struggle.

In this context, it is now possible to identify some of the associations to be stored in the head, the heart, and the bowels of the storyteller. The thought of this story focuses on Jesus' identity: his relationship with John, Moses, and Elijah as the prophets of Israel; his relationship with God, the Father and the Spirit; and his role in relation to Satan and the wild beasts.

The emotions of the story are most intense in the fatherly words of the voice from the heavens to Jesus. Fear is associated with the wild beasts, while the presence of the angels is comforting. The action of the story is a commissioning, an inauguration of a great mission. The gut meaning of the story is then the empowerment and confirmation of Jesus as Messiah. It is the narrative equivalent of an ordination or inauguration. The story invites the listener to experience this event with Jesus, both as an observer and as an intimate co-participant. We, as listeners, are introduced to Jesus of Nazareth intimately and deeply at the beginning of his mission.

Connections

The problem with telling these ancient narratives is that they can continue to be old stories with no relationship to the experience of storytellers and listeners now. Precisely because these are ancient stories, we often find it difficult to understand them sympathetically. For this reason, learning to tell the stories also requires that we explore the ways in which the stories connect with our experience.

There are several experiential connections between this story and our experience that can be explored. I will simply outline a few that you might want to try.

Getting to Know Someone Deeply in a Short Period of Time

It takes very few words in this story to be introduced to Jesus at a deep level. And there are times when we meet or hear about someone and get to know them in a short period of time to a degree of depth that is amazing.

I remember vividly my first evening at Union Theological Seminary in New York. One of my new roommates was Russell Davis, an urbane graduate of the University of Virginia. That night, Russ and I sat up until the early morning telling each other the stories of our lives. We literally got inside each other's heads. And one set of stories we shared was our experiences of being called to ministry. By the end of that evening, we knew each other well. And we have been friends to this day.

The associations of moments like this provide an insight into one of the dynamics of this story. When I tell people about Russ, I tell a couple of his stories from that evening, and others both know him and the closeness of our ties of friendship. By remembering that evening, I know something of the atmosphere I want to generate in telling this story about Jesus of Nazareth.

Experiences of Commissioning, Inauguration, and Ordination

This tradition also connects with experiences of commissioning. In everyone's life there are moments of being launched: graduations, installations, weddings, and baptisms. In those moments, particularly in retrospect, the direction of one's life comes into clear focus. These experiences can both illuminate and be illuminated by the story of Jesus' baptism.

One of the primary functions of these experiences is to empower persons to deal with the fear of the new things that are just ahead. A gift of this story is, therefore, that it can be a resource for persons who are undertaking a new mission or who are facing overwhelming fears. And those two often go together.

The story invites us to experience our own commissionings in the context of Jesus' baptism and testing in the wilderness. In relation to such a time or place in our lives, this story is a gift to be received. It is possible, for example, to pray this story, to enter into it imaginatively in direct relationship with God, the voice, Jesus, the dove. And, as Saint Ignatius of Loyola taught, one can compose that place and time now. To enter into that place and time is to meditate on the event. The story invites us to be there in all the immediacy of each of the senses. The sights, sounds, tastes, touches, and smells of this event in Jesus' life can emerge in prayer. That experience can in turn shed light on our relationship with Christ and on our mission.

Connecting with Present Needs

Listening to the story in relation to one's present needs is another way of connecting with the story. This can happen most naturally with a spiritual companion who is exploring the stories with you. A simple process is to identify the need or situation that this story addresses in our experience and to share that with your friend. Then listen to the biblical story deeply. The role of a spiritual companion here is not to advise or direct but simply to share the story as it is received. If any light or direction emerges from the story, and it feels appropriate, it is good to share that with your friend. But there is no commitment or guarantee. The stories are not magical formulas whose incantation automatically generates light.

A human need addressed in this story is the sense of inadequacy, unworthiness, and fear that accompanies being commissioned for a great mission. If I were going to share that need with a spiritual companion at this moment, it would be in relation to writing this book. I feel inadequate for this task. And I am afraid. My fear is both that I will never accomplish the task and that if I do, it will not be worthy of its purpose. I know the tests that are involved in the process of writing, editing, and publishing a book. If you were with me in this moment, you might choose to tell me the story of Jesus' baptism. And if you are reading this now, you can also know that listening to this story in the centers of myself has set my inadequacies and fears in a new context. The beginning of this mission to which I have been called is now set in the context of Jesus' baptism and testing in the wilderness. I have another companion.

Telling the Story

An essential step in the exploration of a biblical story is to tell it, first to yourself and perhaps to God, then to a partner, to a small group of friends or storytellers, to your primary faith community, and finally to anyone who wants to hear it. The interiorization of the story makes it possible to speak to the interiors of others. Once the story has percolated through the head, the heart, the lower belly, and even down to the toes, it can then come out of your mouth again and resonate fully in the telling. It is now a part of you and can become a story for someone else.

But the most critical element in sharing these stories is to protect the freedom of the listener. Biblical stories are not designed to persuade or to manipulate a listener into agreement. To be sure, there are appeals, and the stories are structured to invite response. But the freedom of the listener to respond in a variety of ways is built into the stories. They do not have only one meaning but open out onto a broad playground of meaning. There the listeners are invited to play.

The playground does have boundaries. It is possible to experience and interpret the stories in ways that are inappropriate to their intent. For example, it is inappropriate to hear this story as an account of Christian triumphalism over Judaism, in which Judaism is somehow superseded by Christianity. The ways in which Jesus' identity as Messiah and Son of God are a fulfillment of Israel's tradition are many and varied. But there is no one meaning or set of principles that can be drawn from this story. It is an invitation to enter into an event.

But every listener has the right to choose whether to hear the story and if so, how. The preservation of the openness of the biblical storytelling tradition is essential to its life. Therefore, with full affirmation of the freedom that God has given you and your listeners, I invite you to tell the story of Jesus' baptism to someone else.

3

HEALING A PARALYTIC

(Mark 2:1-13)

Mark's story of the healing of the paralytic recounts Jesus' action of healing and forgiveness in response to paralysis and radical skepticism. The narrative invites listeners to celebrate both the determined faith of the paralytic and his friends and the joy of his newfound strength to walk. It also welcomes listeners' skepticism about Jesus' authority to act as God who forgives and makes new. The implicit appeal is to have confidence in Jesus as the agent of God's grace and power. The sign of such confidence is an all-out exploration of the possibility of getting up and walking away from whatever cripples us.

Learning the Story with a Group

The best way to get people involved in telling stories is to lead a group through the stages of learning and telling a story. This process leads people through the steps of learning a story, exploring its meaning then and now, and telling it first within and then outside the group. This way of forming oral tradition communities can be done with any group, either all at once or in stages.

Two elements of preparation are essential for the leader. The first is to know the story well. The second is to have copies of the story typed in episodes for every person.

Learning a story with a group is great fun. And the best introduction to learning a biblical story is for people to get physically and emotionally involved as a group in some kind of fun. The essential component is give and take, action and response. A "lion hunt" has become my most frequent starting point, especially with large groups. In a lion hunt, the group says and does everything that the leader says and does, in immediate response. The lion hunt always has the same basic structure. But infinite variations are possible for each particular occasion. The gestures are big and boisterous and can only be learned by doing them. Most camp leaders and kindergarten teachers can initiate you into this august oral tradition. This is an outline:

Hi.
Do you want to go on a lion hunt?
Let's go!
Open the door. Shut the door.
Open the gate. Shut the gate.
Uh oh! Forgot my gun. Gotta go back.
[Repeat door and gate]
Pick up the gun.
Kiss my spouse.
[Repeat door and gate]
Let's go! Great day.
Grass. Medium grass. Tall grass. Low grass. No grass.
Let's climb a tree. Look to the left. Look to the right.
Does anybody see a lion? Nope. Let's go.
Un oh! A river. Big river. Gotta cross.
Does anybody see a bridge? [If so, cross and come to
    another river later.]
Nope. Better get a big run. On your marks, get set,
    GO!
Ooops! Really big river. I'm scared. Crocodiles.

Better get a really big run. On your marks, get set, GO!
Into the river! Swim! Beat off those crocodiles! Swim!
We made it. Way to go!

Mud. Deep mud. Blurp, blurp. Medium mud. Squish,
squish. No mud.

Let's climb another tree. Look to the left. Look to the
right.

Does anybody see a lion? Nope. But there's a cave over
there. Let's go look. Down the tree.

Shh! We're getting close to the cave. And here it is.
Big, dark cave. It's really dark in there.

There's lion tracks goin' in. And there's lion tracks
coming out.

There's human tracks goin' in. But there ain't no
human tracks coming out.

I'm scared. You go first. No, you go first. YOU GO!
Oh, all right, let's go together. Shhh!

Sure is dark in here. Does anybody see a lion? Nope.
I feel something . . . fuzzy.

There's one big yellow eye. There's two big yellow
eyes.

IT'S A LION! RUN!

Up the tree. Down the tree. Through the mud. Into the
river. Up the tree. Down the tree. Through the grass.
Open the gate. Shut the gate. Open the door. Shut the
door. Put up my gun. Kiss my spouse. We made it.
We're home. Way to go! [Clapping]

And, if the group is learning the healing of the paralytic, after
the applause and laughter dies down, go through exactly the
same process with Mark's story. The biblical story needs the
same energy in its words and gestures. Keep the word groups
fairly short. The group says the story back to you with the
gestures.

I would suggest that you imagine yourself with a group and
tell the story back to a leader with total abandon and big
gestures. The more verbal and physical energy you can
generate, the better.

The Story

And when he returned to Capernaum after some days,
  it was reported that he was at home.
And many were gathered together, so that there was no
  longer room for them, not even about the door.
And he was preaching the word to them.

☆   ☆   ☆   ☆   ☆

And they came, bringing to him a paralytic carried by
  four men.
And when they could not get near him because of the
  crowd, they removed the roof above him; and when
  they had made an opening, they let down the pallet
  on which the paralytic lay.
And when Jesus saw their faith, he said to the paralytic,
  "My son, your sins are forgiven."

☆   ☆   ☆   ☆   ☆

Now some of the scribes were sitting there, questioning
  in their hearts, "Why does this man speak like this?
It is blasphemy!
Who can forgive sins but God alone?"

☆   ☆   ☆   ☆   ☆

And immediately Jesus, perceiving in his spirit that
  they were questioning within themselves, said to
  them, "Why do you question like this in your hearts?
What is easier, to say to the paralytic, 'Your sins are
  forgiven,' or to say 'Rise, take up your pallet and
  walk'?
But that you may know that the Son of man has
  authority on earth to forgive sins"—he said to the
  paralytic—"I say to you, rise, take up your pallet and
  go home."

☆   ☆   ☆   ☆   ☆

And he rose, and immediately took up the pallet and
went out before them all.
So they were all amazed and glorified God, saying,
"We never saw anything like this."

After going through the story, analyze its structure. Charting
the episodes on a blackboard or flip-chart is helpful. The group
can suggest a range of possible episode titles. In addition to
naming the episodes, you might also label the sentences and
identify the subjects or key words in each sentence. Keep the
instructions brief and simple. Every word said is a further
interference with the group's short-term memory.

Next, repeat the story again, asking the group to associate
the words with the structure on the chart. Keep the gestures
going so that all three perceptual systems—aural, visual,
kinesthetic—are operative.

Hand out the story in episodes and explain that after the next
round of repetition, each person will tell the story to a partner.
This is a typical introduction:

After I tell it to you and we go through it together again,
I'm going to ask you to turn immediately and tell it to your
partner. The goal will be to get through the story. If you
get lost, your partner will help you. Partners, don't look at
the paper. This paper is dangerous stuff. It can either be a
helper for fledgling storytellers or the primary enemy.
This paper is only an aid to your memory. Don't depend
on it. DON'T LOOK AT IT! Use your memory.
Therefore, while your partners are telling the story,
remember along with them. Listen. If they get lost, just
pick them up at that point. If neither one of you can
remember, then you look and refresh your partner's
memory.

Take these fifteen minutes to tell the story back and
forth as often as you can. Work toward getting through it
with as high a degree of mastery and comfort as possible.
Don't talk about it. We have spent years learning how to
talk about these stories and almost no time learning how

to tell them. Concentrate on the story. If anyone needs help, I'm available.

Our goal is for everyone to be able to get through the story from beginning to end.

After going over the story together once more and perhaps having the leader retell it, the group works on telling the story in groups of two.

It is sometimes helpful to give a group five or ten minutes to work on it individually before telling it to a partner. This has come to be known as the "blab school" method. Everyone tells or reads the story out loud to themselves at the same time. If you include this step, the following instructions may be helpful:

There are some basic rules about this time. First, find your own space. Then tell the story to yourself in a loud voice. Everyone else is going to be telling it too. You'll be fine as long as you tell it loud enough that you can't hear everyone else. But if you are timid and quiet, other people will bother you. Therefore, talk loudly, and you'll be okay. This is going to be organized chaos. Enjoy it! After a few minutes, when I give the signal, find a partner and tell it to each other.

The leader can circulate during this time of one-to-one storytelling and help people who are having difficulties. Many people have difficult emotional and intellectual problems related to storytelling that they need to work through. Some people are sure they can't memorize, or had a traumatic experience with memorization as a child. Others have major reservations about memorizing Bible stories. Others are concerned that they won't remember the story word for word and will get it wrong. However, while a brief discussion may help, it is best not to let people escape into talking about the story rather than telling it. The intellectuals in the group often have the highest degree of resistance. And most of these discussions are avoidance tactics. After a period of ten to fifteen minutes, depending on the length of the story, call the group back. A brief period of feedback is always helpful. The main task is to celebrate the group's achievement.

Learning the Story

Verbal Threads

"Your sins are forgiven." This phrase is the climax of the healing episode and of the scribes' questions, and is picked up in Jesus' question, "What is easier . . . ?" (vss. 5, 9).

"Questioning in their hearts. " This phrase sets the scene for the scribes' questions and Jesus' response (vss. 6, 8). There is a minor variation in the introduction to Jesus' response, "questioning within themselves."

"Rise, take up your pallet." This is the link between Jesus' question to the scribes and his command to the paralytic (vss. 9, 11). The phrase ends first with "and walk," next with "and go home." The thread also ties Jesus' question to the fulfillment of his command: "And *he rose,* and immediately *took up the pallet* [same verbs, different tense in Greek] and went out before them all" (vs. 12).

These verbal threads are typical of the way in which two or three contiguous episodes are woven together. The most frequent connections are (1) the last sentence of one episode and the first of the next, (2) the first and last sentence of the *same* episode, and (3) the first or last sentences of *subsequent* episodes.

Scenes

This story can be visualized as a shooting script for a movie:
Scene 1. Pan shot on the village with the word going out that he's home and people crowding into the house; end with shot through the door to Jesus preaching.
Scene 2. Shot from roof of four coming to the house, going up the steps to the roof, and tearing a hole in the roof; change to shot from floor of the house up to paralytic coming down through the roof and faces of the four; close-up of Jesus and paralytic.
Scene 3. Pan over to scribes sitting on the side; focus in on them talking to each other.

Scene 4. Wide shot of Jesus and the scribes, then close-up of Jesus talking to the paralytic.

Scene 5. Close-up of paralytic getting up; pan back steadily to paralytic walking out, to whole crowd as they respond, and to village again as Jesus and crowd move out to the sea.

Thoughts, Emotions, Actions

The thought of this account focuses on the complex issue of Jesus' authority to forgive sins. The implication of the event is that Jesus is uniquely related to God and to the rest of humanity.

The emotions of the story begin and end with the enthusiasm of the crowd and its attraction to Jesus. The paralytic episode is the most emotionally complex. It moves from the determination of the four, to the surprise and good humor of the roof removal, to Jesus' compassion in response to the paralytic. The emotions of the scribe episode and of Jesus' responses can be variously angry, probing, or satirical, depending on your interpretation.

The story's action connects radical questioning and skepticism with forgiveness, healing, and liberation. It leads the audience into a relationship with the paralytic and his friends and with the scribes as they encounter Jesus. And it calls for a response of joining the crowd in its amazement. The action moves from relaxation/enthusiasm to compassion/tension to expansive release. The effect of the story could be called a catharsis of pity, resignation, and skepticism.

Listening to the Story

The biggest problem in listening to this story in its original context is to discern over the two intervening millennia how Mark presented the dialogue between Jesus and the scribes.

The original context of this story can be clarified by understanding its history as a narrative tradition. Form criticism is a method for the study of biblical narratives in the period of oral formation prior to their being written down. The method involves a detailed comparison of stories with a similar form or structure. These stories are analyzed as a group to determine their typical form and function in oral tradition. The presupposition of this method is that oral traditions are formed and circulated in accordance with patterns or laws of oral transmission. By clarifying the forms or types of stories and sayings in the Synoptic tradition, it is then possible to distinguish the earlier oral forms of a tradition from the later forms in which editing has taken place.

A form-critical analysis of this story is interesting. A typical healing story is composed of a setting and description of the illness, an action that brings the illness to Jesus, a word or action by Jesus, a description of the healing, and a response by the one healed and/or by onlookers. The conflict story is a separate form with its own typical elements. This story is then an unusual combination of the elements of a healing story and the elements of a conflict story.

An examination of Mark's narrative also reveals two clear seams between the earlier and later forms of the narrative. The most readily apparent seam is the highly unusual sentence that ends Jesus' speech to the scribes: "But in order that you may know that the Son of man has authority to forgive sins on earth—he says to the paralytic, I say to you, rise, take up your pallet and go to your house" (literally translated). This sentence is a grammatical nightmare. The first half is a conditional clause addressed to the scribes. In one sense, the sentence is never finished. In mid-sentence, the subject shifts to the paralytic and a new independent clause is introduced. The sentence makes oral sense but only in a somewhat awkward manner. This grammatical incongruity may indicate a seam where two pieces of tradition have been sewn together.

There is evidence of another earlier seam. The subject of the piece that has been sewn in is the dispute between Jesus and the scribes. That piece begins at verse 7, immediately after Jesus' pronouncement of forgiveness. The scribes are somewhat abruptly introduced at this point. There is no mention of scribes in the initial setting of the scene (2:1-2). Assuming that Luke's version of this story (Luke 5:17-26) is later than Mark's, Luke dealt with this problem by making the scribes and Pharisees the main characters in the opening setting and introducing the crowd in the midst of the narrative:

On one of those days, as he was teaching, there were Pharisees and teachers of the law sitting by, who had come from every village of Galilee and Judea and from Jerusalem; and the power of the Lord was with him to heal. (Luke 5:17)

Thus, the narrative patch in Mark's narrative begins with the introduction of the scribes (2:6) and ends with the address to the paralytic (2:10*b*). The earlier form of Mark's story would then have been as follows:

And when Jesus saw their faith, he said to the paralytic, "My son, your sins are forgiven. And I say to you, rise, take up your pallet and go home." And he rose and immediately took up the pallet and went out before them all so that they were all amazed and glorified God, saying, "We never saw anything like this!"

Since this account has the typical form of a healing story—setting, action to bring sickness to Jesus' attention, action/word by Jesus, healing, response—the probability is high that it was an earlier form of the paralytic tradition.

This analysis enables us to see the fascinating way in which the story grew in the telling. The history of the paralytic tradition may also provide some clues about the most serious problem in the telling of this story, namely, how did Mark intend for the scribes' episode to be told? Generally, when this narrative is read aloud today, the scribes are presented as bad guys and the attitude of the reader is distinctly critical. The attitude of the narrator toward the characters of the story is a primary factor in shaping the emotional distance between the listeners and those characters. If the storyteller's attitude toward the scribes is cynical and cutting, the appeal to the listeners will be to separate themselves from the scribes and to regard their questions negatively. The question is whether Mark told the story that way himself and, by implication, intended that we should tell it that way as well.

The tradition history of the paralytic story raises the same question in another form: why did Mark (or a pre-Markan storyteller) add the conflict with the scribes to the story? A thematic reason was to introduce the motif of Jesus' authority to forgive sins. A storytelling answer emerges in telling the story in its earlier form.

Jesus' statement, "Your sins are forgiven," is a radical surprise in the context of first-century Judaism. Not even the high priest had the authority to make such a pronouncement. If Jewish listeners to the original form of the story were shocked by this statement, they may have either stopped listening or have been so offended that they walked away. By including the scribes, who were authorities on such issues, in the story, Mark gave voice to his listeners' questions and wove their response into the story.

If this was the case, Mark presented the words of the scribes sympathetically so that the audience could identify with them. The scribes spoke for them. As a result, when Mark reported Jesus' words in response to the scribes, he spoke directly to the audience as if they were the scribes. In effect, at that moment in the story, the listeners *were* the scribes, listening to Jesus' response to their questions.

As you will see and hear in telling these stories, the impact of biblical narrative depends on this kind of identification with the characters of the story. When the listeners identify with certain characters, the speeches to those characters in the story are addressed to the listeners. The history of this story, with its addition of conflict with the scribes, is congruent with this pattern in the biblical storytelling tradition.

It is easy to see in this context why the attitude of the storyteller now is so important. Contemporary Christian listeners are generally predisposed to be critical of Jews in general and, particularly, of scribes and Pharisees. The history of Christian interpretation of the Gospels has created this predisposition. If there is even the slightest hint of criticism in the storyteller's voice, that will control the audience's attitude. Only if the storyteller presents the scribes' words in a highly sympathetic manner will a contemporary Christian audience identify at all with the scribes and thereby hear the story appropriately. On the other hand, if the story is told with a negative attitude, the effect of the story will be radically changed. It will be experienced as another in a seemingly endless series of human stories in which the effect is to point the finger of ridicule and blame at someone else.

Therefore, Mark probably presented Jesus' words to the

scribes in a sympathetic rather than a critical manner. Likewise, as I hear Mark's telling of this story, the tone of Jesus' words was not hate or disdain but respect and a desire for engagement. Just as Jesus entered into dialogue with the scribes, Mark enters into dialogue with his listeners and asks their questions. I do not see Mark pointing his finger at the audience when Jesus says "But that you may know that the Son of man has authority . . ." but rather opening his hands or touching the side of his head. It is less a confrontation than an invitation.

There was healing and forgiveness in this tale for Mark's listeners, in their identification with the paralytic and with the scribes. This corresponds with the sympathetic dynamics of the story. The first appeal of the story is to identify with the paralytic and his friends in the radicality of their determination to get to Jesus. This identification is the sandwich for the appeal to identify with the scribes in their skepticism. At the conclusion of the story, the implication is that all of them—the crowd and the scribes—glorified God.

Another less complex issue in listening to Mark's story is the report about the roof. How did Mark tell the roof business? (2:4). How big a deal was the hole in the roof? While there is evidence that the mud and stick roofs of ancient Palestine were sometimes opened to let down food, Mark presents it as a radical action. Matthew doesn't even mention the roof. But this is typical of Matthew's extremely concise style in the healing stories. The evidence that Mark made a big deal of the hole in the roof is the number of words he spends on its description. In effect, he describes it twice: "they removed the roof"/"when they had made an opening." However, the Revised Standard Version is a wimpish translation of Mark's Greek. The first phrase literally means "to unroof the roof" while the second verb means "to tear out," here in reference to the mud and sticks of the roof. Often this verb *(eksoruksantes* in Greek) is used to describe tearing out someone's eyes (for examples, see *A Greek-English Lexicon,* Bauer, Gingrich, and Danker 1979, 277). It is a violent word for which "made an opening" is a weak and inept rendering. Thus, Mark probably told this episode in a highly vivid and emphatic manner.

"My son, your sins are forgiven" (vs. 5)—this statement is performative language, similar in its impact and tone to the words declaring a man and woman to be husband and wife. Just as the words "I pronounce you husband and wife" do something significant, so also these words *do* something. They are words which, by their being spoken, cause something to happen. The story focuses down from the high volume and intensity of the tearing open of the roof to these authoritative words of Jesus to the paralytic.

Connections

This story invites us to identify with the paralytic and his friends. In all the healing stories, the audience is invited to sympathize with the one who is afflicted. In this account, the primary focus is on the determination of the friends and the paralytic to get to Jesus.

The story thus invites us to identify our own experiences of being paralyzed and taking radical steps to get help. And, in order to tell the story sympathetically, it is necessary to make that connection. Therefore, a step in learning this story is to remem ber and perhaps tell to yourself or someone else experiences of paralysis and searching for help. When have you been paralyzed by powers beyond your control and asked for help?

As we have seen, the story also invites us to identify with the scribes in their questioning of Jesus and of the possibility that the paralytic can be forgiven. The dynamics of the story require that the storyteller both understand and sympathize with the scribes in their questioning. Who is the scribe in you?

The field of experience that the story addresses is that of defending the rules and customs that have authority in our families and communities. The scribe defends the ways in which things "ought" to be done. While it is important to maintain the specific relationship to the issues addressed in this story, the scribes also represent a type or an attitude that is widely present. Religious people who are threatened by violations of their social and religious customs can identify with the scribes if they will allow themselves to explore their true feelings. There is also a profound skepticism implicit in their questions. Thus, a step in exploring this story is to identify the times when you have felt threatened by the breaking of a social or religious custom or have been radically skeptical about some religious kook's authority. The purpose of this exploration is to find a point of connection with the energy of the scribes' questions.

Telling the Story

A storytelling process has emerged from this story that has proven to be a powerful way of telling and hearing this story. It is a simple and direct way of sharing the story in relation to our personal needs. And I would suggest that you share the story in this way with a storytelling partner.

Share with your partner the ways in which you most deeply identify with the paralytic and the scribe now. In what ways are you paralyzed, unable to move effectively? And in what ways are you skeptical of the possibility that anyone could forgive you and enable you to walk again?

After you have shared, listen to your partner tell you the story. The purpose in telling the story is not to give counsel or spiritual answers, but to share a common faith experience. Telling the story enables us to hear our present experience in the context of Jesus' presence and power. If my partner has shared a present paralysis and skepticism with me, I will respond with the story. And, in the telling, I too will listen for the ways Christ may be present for my friend in this story.

After hearing the story, it is often good to talk about what, if anything, you heard in the story. It may be that you heard nothing and that the story did not connect in any way. And that is perfectly acceptable. Telling these stories does not do something more or less automatically. The stories are words that have the potential to set our experience in the context of the presence of Christ. But if you did hear something that connected with your life, then share and explore it with your partner. Often the stories are meaningful in ways we never could have anticipated.

This process is one of many storytelling possibilities that are available to us. In the aftermath of the accident I mentioned earlier, I was in casts for six months and then unable to walk without a cane for well over a year. There was initially a serious question whether I would be able to walk again. During that period, this story became my story.

I began telling it to myself during the physical therapy in the hospital when I took my first steps between parallel bars: two steps the first day, four the next. But the most frequent tellings were during the months of physical therapy at home. When a knee is immobilized for a long period of time, adhesions grow over the joint. In order to get flexibility back, those adhesions must be broken. The easiest way is to push the joint as hard as you can, gradually breaking them. My task was then to sit and push as hard as I could as long as I could on that joint. After I couldn't stand the pain anymore, I could rest for a few hours before doing the same process again. This went on for months with only small signs of progress.

I told myself this story time after time during this period. Sometimes it was a story of hope. I would envision myself getting up and walking again. Often it was a story of forgiveness: forgiveness for my sins of avoiding or not doing my exercises which alone would enable me to walk again, for my shame at being unable to walk when I had been a runner and a first-rate tennis player, and for my anger at God for not being able to run and play with Tom and Michael, who were then eight and four. It was also a story which gave me a context for exploring my skepticism about ever being able to walk again and about God's ability to enable me to do that. All of my critical and cynical energies as a scholar found expression in the scribes' questions.

Day by day in a variety of ways, I told myself this story and remembered it in exquisite detail. Writing in my journal, prayer, and doing my exercises all became occasions for remembering this story. And in an equally varied number of ways, the story enabled me to recognize and accept Jesus' presence and power.

In the process of remembering this story, Jesus Christ became present for me. Through the story, he welcomed me into the midst of the community in my broken condition, argued with me about the theological issues involved in this stupid accident, and steadily called on me to get up and walk. The return of my strength and energy was a steady gift that was profoundly connected with this story. In some sense, remembering the story enabled me to walk again. For this reason, I would recommend that you open yourself to receiving the unique gifts of this story when you are in stress, pain, or crisis.

4

THE PRODIGAL SON

(Luke 15:11-32)

Jesus' parable of the prodigal son is a story about the relationship between being forgiven and granting forgiveness. The story first draws the listener into condemning a prodigal son. The issue for the listener is then whether to celebrate the prodigal's return to the father or to identify with the elder son in his righteous anger. The impact of the parable is to appeal for the granting of forgiveness.

The Story

And he said, "There was a man who had two sons.
And the younger of them said to his father, 'Father give
    me the share of your property that falls to me.'
And he divided his living between them.

☆   ☆   ☆   ☆   ☆

Not many days later, the younger son gathered all he had
    and took his journey into a far country, and there he
    squandered his property in loose living.
And when he had spent everything, a great famine arose
    in that country.
And he began to be in want.

☆ ☆ ☆ ☆ ☆

So he went and joined himself to one of the citizens of that
country, who sent him into his fields to feed swine.
And he would gladly have fed on the pods that the swine ate.
And no one gave him anything.

☆ ☆ ☆ ☆ ☆

When he came to himself he said, 'How many of my
father's hired servants have bread enough and to
spare, but I perish here with hunger!
I will arise and go to my father, and I will say to him,
"Father, I have sinned against heaven and before
you; I am no longer worthy to be called your son.
Treat me as one of your hired servants." '

☆ ☆ ☆ ☆ ☆

And he arose and came to his father.
But while he was yet at a distance, his father saw him and
had compassion, and ran and embraced him and
kissed him.
And the son said to him, 'Father, I have sinned against
heaven and before you; I am no longer worthy to be
called your son.'

☆ ☆ ☆ ☆ ☆

But the father said to his servants, 'Bring quickly the best
robe, and put it on him, and put a ring on his hand,
and shoes on his feet, and bring the fatted calf and kill
it, and let us eat and make merry.
For this my son was dead, and is alive again; he was lost,
and is found.'
And they began to make merry.

☆ ☆ ☆ ☆ ☆

Now his elder son was in the field.
And as he came and drew near to the house, he heard
music and dancing.

☆ ☆ ☆ ☆ ☆

And he called one of the servants and asked what this
meant.
And he said to him, 'Your brother has come, and your
father has killed the fatted calf, because he has
received him safe and sound.'

☆　☆　☆　☆　☆

But he was angry and refused to go in.
His father came out and entreated him.

☆　☆　☆　☆　☆

But he answered his father, 'Lo, these many years I have
served you, and I never disobeyed your command.
Yet you never gave me a kid, that I might make merry
with my friends.
But when this son of yours came, who has devoured your
living with harlots, you killed for him the fatted calf!'

☆　☆　☆　☆　☆

And he said to him, 'Son, you are always with me, and all
that is mine is yours.
It was fitting to make merry and be glad.
For this your brother was dead, and is alive; he was lost,
and is found.' "

Learning the Story

Verbal Threads

**"This your brother [my son] was dead, and is alive; he was
lost, and is found."** This sentence is the climax of the two halves
of the parable (vss. 24, 32). The only variation is in the
description of the prodigal as "my son" and "your brother."
**"Father, I have sinned against heaven and before you; I am no
longer worthy to be called your son."** The prodigal says these
words first to himself and then to his father (vss. 18, 21). The
variation is that he does not actually ask his father to be taken
back as a hired servant, as he had planned. This omission in

turn adds to the anticipatory silence at the end of the episode prior to the father's ecstatic commands for celebration.

"Kill the fatted calf." This phrase is the primary symbol of the celebration. It is stated first by the father (vs. 23), then the servant (vs. 27), and finally the elder son (vs. 30).

Short Sentences

The relationship between tempo and sentence length can be heard clearly in this parable. The shortness of the sentences and the episodes are indications of tempo and, therefore, of emphasis in the parable as Jesus told it. The general rule in the Gospels is that shortness creates emphasis because the words are said more slowly. In this parable you can get a sense of Jesus' storytelling style.

The first sentences in both halves of the parable are short: "There was a man who had two sons" and "Now his elder son was in the field." And, as I have punctuated the parable, all but one of the final sentences of the episodes in the first half are short (in Greek, six, four, four, seven, nineteen, and three words long). The last is the shortest, "And they began to celebrate" (vs. 24*b*).

Furthermore, the episodes with the shortest sentences are the first and third episodes of the elder brother half of the parable. These describe the elder brother's trip in from the fields (vs. 25) and his angry refusal to go in (vs. 28). The impact of these episodes is also increased by the reduction in episode length from three sentences to two. The slowing down of the tempo in the second half allows more time for the unspoken implications of the elder son's discovery and anger to be savored in the spaces between the words and the episodes. Jesus of Nazareth was clearly a masterful storyteller.

Thoughts, Emotions, Actions

The focus of the parable's thought is the mind of the father. His decisions pose several puzzles: his immediate granting of the son's request for the inheritance without question; his running out and embracing his son before he utters a word; and especially the extravagance of his welcome. Equally puzzling is his willingness to accept the elder son's scathing anger and to beg him to come in. That thought puzzle is the primary riddle of the parable.

The emotions of the story are deep and varied: the prodigal's despair in the pigpen, the shame and grief of his return, the father's joy, the anger of the elder son, and the father's loving plea. Implicit in the episodes describing the prodigal's adolescent excesses is also the deep disgust of the narrator. Identifying this emotional range is helpful in remembering the parable's structure.

The strongest actions of the parable are the interactions between the two sons' actions of repentance and anger and the responses of the father. The parable moves from the joy of the celebration to the impassioned plea of the father. The father's closing gesture is an unspoken appeal to forgive and to join in the celebration. The final action of the parable is left in the hands of the elder son/listener.

Listening to the Story:
An Introduction to Narrative Analysis

The purpose of oral narrative analysis in biblical storytelling is the transferral of the story from one medium to another: from a writing/reading medium to a telling/listening medium. Rather than a trans*form*ation, this could be called a trans*media*zation. In a storytelling event, three factors interact: the storyteller, the audience, and the story. An oral narrative analysis seeks to identify the discrete factors in that interaction so that an appropriate retelling of the written narrative as an oral narrative can take place. The analysis here is organized around the four qualitative components found in Aristotle's *Poetics:* plot, character, thought, and diction.

I will introduce the components briefly. My suggestion would be that you work through an analysis of the parable of the prodigal son, listening for each of these dimensions of the story. Following that analysis, we will work through the parable in detail together, episode by episode. I would encourage you to note those places where your analysis differs from mine. Those differences are the stuff from which the ongoing rediscovery of the story's life will be discovered. You also might want to refer to Ken Parker's worksheet in the Appendix for the narrative analysis on which this outline is based.

1. Plot is the structure of the story's action expressed as a decisive transaction, struggle, or change with assessable consequences in a life. It is the human action of the story. Analysis of plot proceeds in two directions.

a. Episodes—Identify the steps in the story's structure. In the prodigal son, I have already identified the episodes. Notice how each deals with a common subject matter. Also notice each time there is a change in the who, what, where, when, and how of the story. These changes often occur at the beginning of a new episode. Pay attention to any structural parallels between the beginning and ending of the story as a whole, between sections within the story, and between individual episodes.

b. Structure—Identify the overall sequence of events within which the story is placed. Where does this story fit in the overall sequence? What is the impact of this story upon the stories that precede and follow it? In what ways is it related to other stories in the Gospel? In particular, look at the book as a whole and at the section of the book in which the story occurs.

Next, listen for and note the internal structure of events in which the story is developed. What signs of tensions and resolutions are present? What is the impact of this tension/resolution sequence on the listener?

2. Character is the building of the story's characters, by which they are ascribed moral qualities. This is often based on what they seek or avoid. It is the interpersonal, human motivation of the story. There are at least three dimensions of characterization that can be identified:

a. Perspective/point of view—At some points in the story, the story's action will shift from an "objective" description of the action from an observer's perspective to a "subjective" description from a character's perspective. These "inside views" may describe a character's sense perceptions, generally of what has been seen or heard. (Descriptions of taste, touch, or smell are also inside views, but they occur infrequently in biblical narrative.) An even deeper inside view may describe a character's feelings, either directly or indirectly. These changes in narrative perspective have a great impact on the listener's relationship to the character because the events are experienced from the character's point of view. An inside view can show the listeners what is inside a character's head and heart.

b. Narrative comments—A narrator can also intervene directly in the story by making a narrative comment to the audience. In biblical stories, narrative comments are generally used to give additional information about something puzzling in the story.

c. Norms—The norms of judgment in a story are the criteria of good and bad, right and wrong, that provide the basis for the storyteller's implicit appeals to the listeners. Norms are often indirectly expressed in the attitudes of the narrator. In a biblical story, we are listening to the story event and seeking to discern the norms of the ancient storytellers and their listeners. In telling the story now, a primary problem is to translate those values so that they can be experienced by contemporary listeners. For example, what are the norms in this parable in relation to pigs? How can they be translated for twentieth-century midwestern farmers? What are the norms in this story for what is good and bad, right and wrong, happy and unhappy?

d. Distance—A primary factor in human relationships is emotional distance, which can range from intimacy and identification to hostility and alienation. In a good story, these dynamics of distance change constantly in the listener's relationship to the various characters. What are the dynamics of distance in this parable in relation to the prodigal son, the father, and the elder son? How do the dynamics of distance change?

3. Thought is the expression of the story's ideas. These ideas may either be intellectual presuppositions shared between the narrator and the audience, or they may be introduced in the story. Often the thought of a story is based on listener expectations in relation to a certain idea, which are then reversed as in the story of the paralytic. Analysis of thought pays attention to the suspense and surprise in a story's development. In this parable, the central thought is the kingdom of God. What does the parable assume about the listeners' ideas about the kingdom of God and how are these ideas reinforced and reversed? What elements of suspense and surprise are built into the parable around these ideas?

4. Diction is the communication of the story's plot, characters, and thought through the verbal and nonverbal behaviors of the storyteller. It is the actual communication of the storyteller. Analysis of diction listens for matters such as tempo, volume, verbal threads, and gesture.

a. Verbal threads—The repetition of words and phrases is the basic linking technique in oral narrative. These function as mnemonic devices as well as imaginative patterns. Listen for the repetition of words both within the story and with the stories that precede and follow it in the larger narrative. Concordance study is an indispensible tool for this research. Listen for associations and connotations, for what is heightened, reversed, and reshaped.

b. Gestures—While we have no explicit record of the gestures in the text, there are gestures implicit in the story. For example, what gestures are implied in the episodes that describe the prodigal returning to his father and the father calling to his servant? The elder son's anger and the father's response?

From the conclusions of this analysis, the actual shaping of a telling of the story will be developed. Three general guidelines for rendering the story are as follows:

1. Adapt delivery verbally and nonverbally to the story's character.

2. Achieve clarity for the audience by alternate wordings and, where needed, brief explanations.

3. Avoid trivialization by keeping metaphorical terms and the primary narrative forms. In particular, don't trivialize the story by describing what it means or by giving a moral unless it is in the story itself.

The following analysis of the parable of the prodigal son is presented in a more detailed manner so that you can see how the study of a biblical text as an oral narrative might be done.

Episode 1 (15:11-12)

The norms of judgment operative in the evaluation of the request of the younger son are the major issue of this episode. Kenneth Bailey has the most illuminating treatment of this issue. He cites extensive evidence from both ancient Jewish literature and from modern Middle Eastern culture in support of his contention that "the prodigal is shown as wishing for his father's death in his request for his portion" (Bailey 1976, 161). He reports that he has discussed this issue with people throughout the Middle East. Almost universally, when asked what it would mean if a son were to make this request of his father, the response has been that the request means he wants his father to die. The degree of emotional shock such a request implies today is clearly indicated by the only two instances Bailey found of a son actually making such a request. They are so revealing about the dynamics of the norms of judgment in this episode that they deserve extensive quotation:

In the first case Pastor Viken Galoustian of Iran, with a convert church of Oriental Jews, reported to me that one of his leading parishioners, in great anguish, reported to him, "My son wants me to die!" The concerned pastor discovered that the son had broached the question of the inheritance. Three months later the father, a Hebrew Christian (a physician), in previously good health, died. The mother said, "He died that night!" meaning that the night the son dared to ask for his inheritance the father "died." The shock to him was so great that life was over that night. In the second case a Syrian farmer's *older* son asked for his inheritance. In great anger his father drove him from the house. (Bailey 1976, 162)

While it is open to question whether this is conclusive evidence in relation to the first century, customs in the Middle East have not changed markedly in this regard. There is a key passage from the Mishna *(Baba Bathra* viii. 7) that reads:

If one assign in writing his property to his children, he must write, "from today and after (my) death." . . . If one assign in writing his estate to his son (to become his) after his death, the father cannot sell it since it is conveyed to his son, and the son cannot sell it because it is under the father's control. . . . The father may pluck up (produce) and feed it to whomsoever he pleases, but whatever he left plucked up belongs to his heirs. (Bailey 1976, 164)

This tradition of the father passing the inheritance while he was still healthy carried with it the right of benefitting from the property until his death; he continued to enjoy the "usufruct."

Thus, while the son obtains the right of possession, he does not have the right to dispose of the property (Jeremias 1962, 128-29; Bailey 1976, 163).

The immediate effect of the characterization of the younger son is, therefore, to make him a highly alien character. The father's granting the request is itself somewhat surprising. There is a strong possibility, as indicated by the instance of the Syrian farmer quoted earlier, that Jesus' listeners would have expected the father to throw the son out of the house in anger. But Jesus presents the father as one who simply observed the custom and divided the inheritance between them. The younger son's share of the inheritance was probably one-third; the elder son's two-thirds.

Episode 2 (15:13-14)

The son's actions go quickly from bad to worse. The implication of the first sentence of the second episode is that he not only asked for ownership of the property but also demanded the right of disposal. Only if he had received this right could he have sold the property. This is still another level of offense against his father and the family. Sale of the family's land was an extremely radical and offensive action. And the implication of the phrase "far country" is that he went to Gentile territory. While the son's disposal of the property was offensive, his use of the money multiplies the offense. To spend the family's inheritance in a Gentile country would certainly have been judged very negatively by Jesus' Palestinian listeners. Furthermore, he spent the money in loose living.

There may be a note of some irony in Jesus' report that a famine arose in that land. Famines were relatively frequent in Palestine and one of the reasons why persons emigrated was in order to avoid these crises. It may well be that Jesus is appealing here for a response such as "It serves him right!" A certain gloating at the misfortune of hometown kids who try to make it in the big city and end up in trouble is a relatively timeless phenomenon.

There is no necessary implication in the phrase usually translated as "loose living" that he spent the money immorally.

The only exegetical basis for this reading is the older brother's later statement that he wasted the inheritance with prostitutes. The *Theological Dictionary of the New Testament* explains the phrase in this manner: "The dissipated life of the Prodigal . . . is simply depicted as carefree and spendthrift in contrast to the approaching dearth" (vol. 1, 507). Jesus may intentionally imply that the elder son read his brother's behavior in the worst possible light. But this in no way minimizes the offensiveness of the young man's actions for Jesus' listeners.

Episode 3 (15:15-16)

The word usually translated "to join" means "to join together, cling, closely associate." Bailey notes that "in the Middle East the desperation of the indigent leads him to attach himself like glue to any potential benefactor" (Bailey 1976, 170). And this Gentile gave him the most repulsive job for a Jewish boy: a pig herder. The degree of revulsion that Jews had for swine is difficult for us to feel. Swine were seen as unclean animals. Associating with them made the young man unclean and, therefore, unable to practice his religion in any way (Jeremias 1962, 129). By taking this job, he becomes virtually a traitor to Judaism. Thus, it is written in the Mishnah, tractate *Baba Kamma* viii. 7, "Cursed be the man who would breed swine." In order for us to feel the degree of revulsion this description had for Jesus' listeners, it is necessary to combine the associations of the most repulsive animals (bats, rats, snakes) and symbols of national desecration (flag burning, active collaboration with the enemy).

The question of why he did not eat the carob pods has been answered variously. According to Bailey, some types of carob pods were and continue to be eaten in the Middle East, particularly during periods of famine. *Ceratonia siliqua,* which is usually identified with the material described here, is widely eaten (1976, 173). Bailey's answer is that Jesus was referring to a wild variety of *kharnub* that was bitter to the taste. My sense of this sentence is that Jesus is describing the young man's internal agony of being so hungry that he wanted to eat the swine's food but that he would not because the idea was so repulsive. Imagine wanting to eat the food that one was feeding to a repulsive animal such as a rat or a snake. The revulsion is associated with becoming like that animal by eating the same food.

The final short sentence of the episode describes his desperation as a starving Jew in a Gentile country. The only other source of food would have been a gift. But in a time of famine an alien like him was not a likely candidate for charity.

Episode 4 (15:17-19)

The description of his turning inside himself is similar to other introductions to an inside view in Jesus' parables (e.g., the introduction to the rich man, Luke 12:17; also Luke 16:3). They have the same structure: a question regarding a present problem followed by an action decision. In each instance the inside view creates greater sympathy. This is the turning point in the distance relationship to the young man. Prior to this, every new statement about his actions or thoughts has heightened the hostile and alienating aspects of his characterization. Even the insight into his wanting to eat the carob pods is repulsive in its impact. But here the dynamics change.

A major question in relation to the young man's speech is whether it really signifies a repentance. After all, he rightly recognized that he was starving to death and that he had burned his bridges when he left; he had in fact given up every right of sonship. Now he is only acknowledging what is perfectly evident to everyone. As Bailey has stated: "From a Jewish understanding of repentance, . . . the prodigal's motivation in the far country is suspect and needs some verification. The motivation is hunger. If he had been financially successful, he would not have considered returning home" (Bailey 1976, 176).

This is a problem of norms of judgment. We tend to equate righteousness with unselfishness, the renunciation of self-interest. As a result, we are tempted to conclude that when the son calculates his own advantage, he is being selfish. Since he goes back in order to save his own skin, he is not really repenting. My conclusion is that neither Jesus nor his audience would have regarded acting in self-interest as bad. Jesus continually appeals to enlightened self-interest in his teachings (e.g., the parables of the dishonest steward, the rich fool, the rich man and Lazarus, the ten virgins, the talents, and the Last Judgment). His question is, do you act wisely in your own interest in light of the coming of the kingdom of God, or do you act stupidly? Jesus assumes that his listeners are smart, calculating persons who are trying to live. A continual question underlying the parables is, in the light of the coming kingdom of God, what is in your best interest? Jesus does not present the calculation of personal self-interest as wrong. But since we have come to understand the absence of calculation as the essence of true repentance, we often tend to read that norm of judgment back into the parables.

The young man's internal dialogue is not set in a context of negative evaluation. He is making a realistic assessment of the situation. Jesus appeals here for a change from alienation to sympathy in relation to the son.

Furthermore, Jesus' listeners knew the degree of humiliation that would be involved in such a return. His resolution to go home and confess to his father includes a realistic assessment of his offense against not only his father but also the entire community. For the prodigal to go home a failure will mean humiliation and mockery. Indeed, he will probably be rejected—even by his father. That is, Jesus' listeners would have known well the consequences of such a return. The son will have to "eat humble pie." Thus, the evidence indicates that Jesus presented the young man as being willing to accept this degree of humiliation. Jesus is here describing repentance, a turning around and a seeking of reconciliation with the father.

His statement itself is repentant in nature. He resolves to make a total confession to his father. The two objects of his sin, "against God and before you," are named explicitly, as is the appropriate judgment, the loss of the rights of sonship. This speech stands in total contrast to the son's first statement to his father. Both begin with the same word, "Father." And both end with an imperative. But the first has a tone of arrogance while the second sounds a note of pleading, of humble request. And his request is that he be given the lowest position in the family's hierarchy. The depth of this statement is awesome. He had declared his independence. For him now to turn around and accept this humble position in relation to his father is the essence of repentance.

Note the order of his description of his sin—"against heaven and before you." The connotations of these phrases are eschatological and cultic. To sin against heaven is to ally oneself with those cosmic powers that struggle against the powers of heaven. He has set himself against heaven, against the powers of the new age. The phrase "before you" is cultic language that is associated with being before God (for example, Exod. 3:6; 22:8-9; 34:20, 23). The implication is that he has committed this sin publicly in the sight of his father. Thus, his projection of his confession is a full and open statement of his action with no equivocation or attempt to hide what he has done.

The statement regarding his sonship builds upon the central importance of the name in Hebrew culture. The power of the name was at the heart of identity, for God and for each person. "Hallowed be Thy name" states the basic hope that God's name will be honored and respected by all. Thus, to give up one's name is to give up one's identity. And, in the first century, one's name was composed of a first name and one's father's name, for example, Simon bar-Jonah—Simon, son of John. His statement is then that he is no longer worthy to bear the family's name. To have lost the inheritance is serious. But to lose one's name is to lose everything. We speak of seeking to "clear my name." For Jesus' audience, this degree of voluntary confession was extreme.

Finally, the question has been raised about the degree of status that he requested in asking to be treated as a hired hand. Bailey has argued that this was a position of some stature, and that the son in requesting this position was planning to ask for a degree of freedom and independence that he later rejected during the actual meeting with his father. Thus, he sees the true act of repentance as coming only in the actual speech to the father in which he gives up any requests and simply throws himself upon his father's mercy (Bailey 1976, 177-79). Bailey then argues that Jesus presents the young man as still calculating a face-saving position in planning to make this request. My sense of the younger son's plan to ask his father to treat him as a hired hand is that he was asking to be seated at the last chair at the banquet. He is projecting a willingness to accept the lowest position. It is then a climactic expression of his willingness to accept permanently a position of humility in relation to his father and in contrast to his former position.

Episode 5 (15:20-21)

The younger son immediately acts upon his decision. In my mind, the picture of the return has generally been on a prairie-like place with a farm house out in the middle of some fields; the father runs down a long road to embrace his son. Bailey's argument is that Jesus' listeners would have known that homes, even of large landholders, were generally in town. Their picture would have been of the father going out to meet him at the edge of the village.

The highly expressive word which describes the father's feeling upon seeing his son is *splagnizomai,* which, as was noted earlier, literally means "to turn over the bowels, to have pity or compassion." This is an inside view of the father's feelings as he sees his son.

Bailey's comments about the surprising character of the father's running to greet his son are delightful:

An oriental nobleman with flowing robes never runs anywhere. To do so is humiliating. A pastor of my acquaintance was not accepted as the pastor of a particular church because in the judgment of the elders, he walked down the street too fast. This custom is preserved even in a modern Middle Eastern metropolis by the Orthodox priest who, of course, still wears the long robes and is careful to walk at a slow, dignified pace. (Bailey 1976, 181)

The father is presented by Jesus as one who is unconcerned about custom or humiliation in his compassion and love for his son. The kiss is a sign of forgiveness (see, e.g., II Sam. 14:33).

Jesus makes the actual doing of the confession even more humbling than its contemplation. The impact of the son's speech is created by the comparison to what he had planned to say. The speech is begun just as planned. But he leaves off the last request for a position as a hired hand. Most commentators have assumed that the absence of the final line was caused by the father's interruption, which does not allow the son to finish. In that instance, Jesus would not have paused between the son's statement and the father's response. But the episode divisions indicate that Jesus made a major pause after the son's confession. In this case, the impact of the absence of the last line is that the younger son renounces the possibility of asking for anything and throws himself upon his father's mercy.

The elements of exaggeration in Jesus' parables are of crucial importance. My hypothesis is that the elements of exaggeration (hyperbole) or total reversal of expectations are those points in the parables at which the story ceases to be about something that could have happened in a Galilean village in A.D. 30–33 and becomes a metaphor of the kingdom of God. Until that point of exaggeration or reversal, the listener can interpret the story in relation to this world. But once the story's plausibility cracks, it ceases to be a realistic description of an actual event and becomes a parable, a metaphor of the kingdom.

The first point of hyperbole in this story is the father's running to greet his son. No father in the experience of Jesus' listeners would have greeted a delinquent son in this manner. It is an exaggeration of affection beyond belief.

Episode 6 (15:22-24)

But the father's homecoming celebration for his son is the parable's greatest exaggeration. The celebration is beyond all appropriate proportions. The episode is filled with allusions to the eschatological banquet. The image of the robe has eschatological connotations (e.g., see Isa. 61:10; Rev. 4:4; 7:9, 14; 22:14). For example, in Mark 2:21 Jesus compares the Messianic Age to a new garment. The ring was probably understood to be a signet ring, a sign of authority. Thus, in Genesis 41:42 the gift of the ring and festal garments is a sign that Joseph is invested with Pharaoh's powers. The shoes were a sign of his being a free man in the house rather than a servant (cf. Jeremias 1962, 189). The killing of the calf rather than a goat or a lamb means that this is a major celebration such as would happen only for the marriage of the eldest son, the visit of the governor of the province, or some other grand occasion. The son is treated, therefore, as a guest of honor. The traditions of hospitality and grand celebration are combined with the granting of all the symbols of authority. It is probable that Jesus told it in a grand manner with exaggeration of voice and manner.

Episode 7 (15:25)

The elder son's entry into the story is presented slowly and with an extensive inside view describing what he heard. The effect of the episode for the listeners is that unique delight or agony of knowing something that someone else is about to discover, such as the birth of a child or the death of a loved one. The music and dancing refer to the celebration that followed the feast. The norms of judgment are all positive in relation to the elder son. He has been working and his discovery of the celebration builds the anticipation of his response.

Episode 8 (15:26-27)

The elder son's realization of what has happened is narrated in a straightforward manner. It may be that the servant's report is given in that unique tone of one who knows that he has news that will make the recipient very upset.

Episode 9 (15:28)

The most intimate insight into the elder son's feelings is the description of his outrage and refusal to enter. As Bailey points out, this was a serious offense, since he was expected to be present. The father's coming out to him is humiliating to the father, as are all such public demonstrations of inner family conflicts in the Middle East. However, the elder son is at this point still a very sympathetic character. Throughout these three episodes, the slowing down of the tempo of the parable gives the listener time to consider the full implications of the elder son's discovery from his point of view.

The father's response to the elder son is to beg him to come in. Once again, he chooses to humble himself for the sake of his son.

Episode 10 (15:29-30)

The elder son insults his father by omitting the term of address. This is the first negative action of the elder son. His accusation is a classic statement from the perspective of the Deuteronomic theology of reward for the righteous and punishment for the wicked. The two sentences are in antithetical parallelism:

The elder son	*The younger son*
a. I have slaved for you and never disobeyed.	a. This son of yours has squandered the inheritance on whores.
b. I have never been given even a goat.	b. You kill for him the fatted calf.

The elder son's speech is a scathing attack on his father's integrity. He accuses him of an exact reversal of justice. His logic is sound, but his attitude toward his father is in marked contrast to his brother's attitude.

In the course of the speech, he dissociates himself from the family. He omits his father's title, identifies himself as a slave rather than a son, identifies his brother as "this son of yours," and states that his idea of a celebration would be to have a party with his friends rather than with the family. A primary norm of judgment in Jesus' culture was family solidarity. It is possible that the elder son's outrage was somewhat offensive to Jesus' listeners. In the recital of this episode, therefore, the most appropriate manner is probably an excessive anger, cutting and extremely insulting in tone. The exegesis would indicate that some distance was created from the elder brother in this speech.

Episode 11 (15:31-32)

The father uses the title of affection, literally meaning "child," which was used, for example, by Jesus in addressing the paralytic (Mark 2:5). He assures the elder son of his rights by describing the actual situation in relation to the inheritance at this point. Since he had already divided the inheritance and given his sons ownership, everything that the father had belonged to his son. His defense is a repetition of the initial statement announcing the celebration. It is necessary to celebrate because of the greatness of this victory. It is an appeal for recognition of the necessity of celebration. The most poignant moment in the speech is his reversal of the name the elder son used for the younger son, from "this son of yours" to "your brother." The unspoken appeal at the end of the parable is to forgive both of them and to join the celebration.

Since the story has been established as a parable during the episode of the banquet, the paradox at the end of the parable is that the younger son is sitting at the eschatological banquet, forgiven and included in the family. The elder brother is, by his own decision, sitting outside the banquet, outraged at the injustice he has suffered and alienated from his family.

The major issue in the historical interpretation of this parable is whether this parable was told by Jesus to the Pharisees and other critics of his ministry in defense of his practice of eating with sinners and tax collectors, or whether this was a parable of proclamation of the kingdom of God. Generally, this parable has, when interpreted as a parable of the kingdom of God, focused on the younger son. Thus, many ministers who preach on this parable leave out the entire section on the elder son. The parable is thereby interpreted as a proclamation of the forgiveness of repentant sinners. However, when this parable has been heard with the elder son section, as Jesus intended, the focus of attention has often shifted in allegorical manner to an identification of those who are like the elder son. Thus, the conclusion has often been that Jesus was addressing those who would be most like the elder son, namely, Jesus' critics and those who were primarily concerned about the observance of the law, namely, the Pharisees.

My conclusion is that the whole parable was intended for the common folk of Galilee. A central dynamic of the parable was to make clear the relationship between forgiveness and the kingdom of God. The parable does these things:

1. The first episodes of the parable create total alienation from the younger son. The appeals for condemnation in the

first three episodes of the parable are extremely radical and polemical in character.

2. The younger son's repentance and return is presented from a sympathetic inside view; the appeal is for recognition and acceptance of his repentance. But the expectation of Jesus was that his listeners would continue to be somewhat skeptical and reserve any major reversal of judgment. The degree of shift is too briefly developed to enable such a total transformation of judgment to take place.

3. The father's welcome of the son both prior to and especially after his confession is exaggerated and goes beyond what any earthly father would do. His extravagant reception and the signs of authority and power that he gives to his son are all analogous to the investiture of the children of God which was expected in the Messianic Age. The impact of this is then a total reversal of expectations. The appeal in the parable is to join the celebration. But the norms of judgment that would make that possible are not fully established and reinforced in the parable itself. The father's response is beyond all possible righteousness and is so excessive as to be unbelievable.

4. The norms of judgment in relation to the elder son are thoroughly believable and present in the audience. The degree of identification with the elder son in his discovery of the celebration and his subsequent anger is very high. Jesus appeals for identification with one who has been treated unfairly by a father. At the same time, the recognition of the negative and embarrassing character of the elder son's action in refusing to go in may well be implicit in the story.

5. The elder son's speech is sympathetic but excessive. The degree of his dissociation from the family and his insults to both his father and his brother are severe. Nevertheless, the father's response is not a condemnation of the elder son but is rather an appeal to him to recognize the justice of the situation in relation to both his own position and that of his brother. It is an appeal to accept his brother again as a member of the family.

6. The paradox at the end of the parable is that the prodigal son is sitting at the banquet of the kingdom of God. In the language of the parable, he is in. The elder son is out.

The parable's dynamics involve a double reversal. The

listener's relationship to the younger son begins in total alienation and moves to a high degree of sympathy. On the other hand, the relationship to the elder son begins in sympathy and ends with critical distance. As a parable of the kingdom, the parable is a total reversal of expectations: the sinner is in and the righteous one is out. The key to understanding and experiencing the parable's dynamics is in the norms of judgment that control the attitudes toward the sons.

The most direct connection in Jesus' teaching with this parable occurs in the Lord's Prayer: "Forgive us our debts, as we also have forgiven our debtors" (Matt. 6:12). Jesus continually teaches the inextricable relationship between forgiving others and the possibility of receiving forgiveness oneself. There is no possibility of receiving forgiveness without also giving it. The parable of the unforgiving servant (Matt. 18:23-35) is another instance of this same theme in Jesus' teaching. The paradox of the prodigal son parable is that the elder son chooses not to participate in the banquet because of his sense of injustice and his unwillingness to forgive his brother. Thus, this parable was and is addressed to all those who find it difficult to forgive others and to accept forgiveness themselves.

It is very clear that the parable celebrates repentance and the granting of forgiveness. It is an attack on those attitudes that might lead us not to forgive and to miss our own needs for forgiveness. It is an appeal for the justice and righteousness of forgiveness in relation to all the enemies of righteousness. The proclamation of the kingdom is then the necessary interrelationship between one's own forgiveness and entry into the kingdom and the granting of forgiveness to others. The direction of distance in relation to the elder son is, however, in the opposite direction as that of the younger son. The parable creates alienation from the elder son. It forces reflection upon the paradox of his response.

Thus, while the parable could undoubtedly have been meaningful to the Pharisees as a defense of Jesus' ministry to sinners and as an appeal for the Pharisees' recognition of the rightness of that ministry, my assessment is that the parable was addressed to a much more general and universal situation.

Jesus' listeners were primarily common folk in Galilee, men and women who would be able to understand and participate fully in this story. The problem Jesus was addressing in this parable is one he addresses frequently: condemnation is catching. If we condemn others, we condemn ourselves. And if we have been forgiven, we must forgive others. We all are both the prodigal son and the righteous son; so were the Pharisees. Jesus addresses the paradox in the relationship that all of us as individuals and as groups have to the kingdom of God.

Connections

An essential part of telling biblical stories is to identify with the story. Detachment is fine for scholarship, but a dispassionate telling is generally deadly. A helpful metaphor is that of a vase. The words of the story are a vase, a container into which our experience can be poured. Thus, one way of exploring the story is to identify experiences in your own life that have the same dynamics or emotions. These connections may help you find an oral interpretation of the words that is real for you. It is one way of making these ancient words your own.

Take, for example, the swine in this story. Imagine the animals that are the most repulsive to you: rats, roaches, bats, snakes, or whatever. The image in the story is that you would be eating the same food with them. Then describe that imagined experience with full emotional intensity.

Another approach would be to think of the most repulsive association with food you have ever experienced. I remember when we moved into our first parsonage in an inner-city metropolitan church. The house had not been lived in for some months except by persons who would sleep there for a night or two. We went to the grocery store and came back with things to put in the refrigerator. When we opened the refrigerator, there was food oozing with green and yellow mold, and maggots were crawling out of the food all over the walls of the refrigerator. It was literally crawling with bacteria. All I have to do is to think of that refrigerator and I know how to tell the episode about the swine. The younger son was so hungry that he wanted to eat the food from that refrigerator. There were also rats in the house. For me, another ready connection is that he wanted to eat the garbage that the rats ate in the adjoining lots. By telling the story of the maggots or the rats to myself or a friend, I can discover the connection that will enable me to tell the episode of the swine convincingly.

A second area of possible connections is with repentance. The young man in the story has to swallow his pride, recognize the great wrong he has done, and project what he would do and say if he went home. The connection is with experiences of shame. Many of these most vivid experiences are rooted in childhood. Some memory of coming home and publicly acknowledging something of which you were deeply ashamed will help to give the young man's words meaning for you. It is not necessary to change the words. In fact, the words of the biblical story can provide a healthier context for those memories than telling your story directly.

Other possible connections are with joy and anger. The father's joy at the return of the prodigal is wholly excessive. It is total ecstasy. The moments of greatest joy in your life are your connection with the story. The elder son's realization of what his father has done for his brother creates in him the ultimate rage. When have you been angry and jealous that someone else has received an award or privilege that you wanted or deserved?

Telling the Story

There are many contexts in which to tell the story. And the parable of the prodigal son opens many contexts for reflection. But the primary action of the parable is to connect with our experiences of needing forgiveness from God and needing to grant forgiveness to others. A way both to hear and to tell this parable is, therefore, to be open to hearing this story of Jesus in relation to those present realities.

Either for yourself or a group, these questions can provide a context for telling the parable: When have you been forgiven?

When have you found it difficult to forgive someone else? In what ways are you now in need of forgiveness? Whom do you need now to forgive? The focus of these questions can be either personal or communal. That is, the persons who come to mind may be either individuals or groups of people. To tell the story to oneself or to someone else may be an occasion that will shed new light on this relationship. The telling of the parable itself can be a time when the real presence of the kingdom of God is made clear. In the silence that follows the father's plea, the question is, how will we complete the parable?

5

WALKING ON THE WATER

(Matthew 14:22-33)

This story addresses the primal fears that cripple us as human beings and as followers of Jesus. These are fears of the power of chaos in its many and varied forms, from the uncontrollable powers of nature to the irrational forces that suddenly arise from the depths of our personal and communal lives. Symbolized as storms, wind, and ghosts, these unknown forces of chaos blow through our lives. And the fear of these powers often leads us into weak resignation, cowardice, and withdrawal. This story is an experience of testing those powers, discerning who is truly in control, and taking the first steps toward true discipleship. It sets those fears in the context of Jesus' power, which he both exercises on our behalf and offers to those who believe in him.

The Story

And immediately he made the disciples get into the boat
   and go before him to the other side, while he
   dismissed the crowds.
And after he had dismissed the crowds, he went up into
   the hills by himself to pray.

☆   ☆   ☆   ☆   ☆

93

When evening came, he was there alone.

But the boat by this time was many furlongs distant from
the land, beaten by the waves.

For the wind was against them.

☆ ☆ ☆ ☆ ☆

And in the fourth watch of the night he came to them,
walking on the sea.

But when the disciples saw him walking on the sea, they
were terrified, saying, "It is a ghost!"

And they cried out from fear.

☆ ☆ ☆ ☆ ☆

But immediately he spoke to them, saying, "Take heart,
it is I.

Have no fear."

And Peter answered him, "Lord, if it is you, bid me come
to you on the water."

He said, "Come."

☆ ☆ ☆ ☆ ☆

So Peter got out of the boat and walked on the water and
came to Jesus.

But when he saw the wind, he was afraid.

And beginning to sink he cried out, "Lord, save me."

☆ ☆ ☆ ☆ ☆

Jesus immediately reached out his hand and caught him,
saying to him, "O man of little faith, why did you
doubt?"

And when they got into the boat, the wind ceased.

And those in the boat worshiped him, saying, "Truly you
are the Son of God."

Learning the Story

Verbal Threads

The major thread that ties this story together is fear: "They
cried out from fear" (vs. 26) is the climax of the fourth-watch

episode; the end of Jesus' response is, "Have no fear" (vs. 27); and finally, "When [Peter] saw the wind, he was afraid" (vs. 30).

"Walking on the sea [waters]." The first two sentences of the central episode have the same key phrase, "he came to them, walking on the sea" (vs. 25) and "[they] saw him walking on the sea" (vs. 26). A variation of the same phrase describes Peter walking on the water (vs. 29), which in turn picks up the key word in Peter's request to Jesus, "bid me come to you on the water" (vs. 28).

"The boat." Jesus commands them to get into the boat (vs. 22); the boat is many yards from shore, beaten by the waves (vs. 24); Peter gets out of the boat (vs. 29); and after the rescue, Jesus and Peter climb up into the boat (vs. 32). The boat is the central motif at or near the beginning of the first and last of the story (vss. 22-23, 31-33). Thus, getting into, out of, and up into the boat is a verbal thread that knits together the framing scenes of the story.

"Dismissed the crowd." The first two sentences of the story are connected by this phrase: "while he dismissed the crowd" (vs. 22) and "after he had dismissed the crowd" (vs. 23).

"Bid me come"/"come." In the same manner, Peter's request "bid me come" (vs. 28) is followed by Jesus' call, "Come" (vs. 29).

The episodes of this story have the characteristic marks of episode beginnings that describe either the time or the place of the action: (1) "immediately," (2) "when evening came," (3) "in the fourth watch," (4) "immediately," (6) "got out of the boat," (7) "immediately." These openings both set the scene for each new episode and tie it to the preceding one. These connections make remembering the episodes of the story a simple step-by-step process.

The two parts of the story have a common three-part structure: walking on the water, first by Jesus (vs. 25ff.) and then Peter (vs. 29); a response of fear and crying out by the disciples (vs. 26) and then Peter (vs. 30); and Jesus' immediate response, which calms their fears (vss. 27, 31-32).

Listening to the Story

A comparison of the different ways in which Mark and Matthew tell this story is interesting. Mark presents this story as a theophany that reveals Jesus' divine character. Mark's puzzling inside view of Jesus intending to "pass by them" is related to the frequent motif in the stories of Moses and Elijah of the revelation of God "passing by" (Exod. 33:19, 22; I Kings 19:11). Matthew has included in this story other elements from the Old Testament traditions of divine appearances. "It is I" is a translation of the Greek *ego eimi,* which is the name of God in the theophany at the burning bush (Exod. 3:14). Translating this phrase as "I am" more clearly preserves this connection to the divine name. Also, "have no fear" is a characteristic motif in stories of appearances by a divine figure, either God or angels (Gen. 15:1; Judg. 6:23; Dan. 10:12; Luke 1:13; 2:10). These motifs in Matthew are the most explicit characterization of Jesus as a divine figure to this point in the narrative. But the most distinctive element of Matthew's telling of the story is Peter's courageous, if short-lived, walking on the water. This transferral of Jesus' divine power to Peter is Matthew's unique contribution to this narrative tradition.

The story has an unusually complex setting that requires two episodes to get everything in place. The first episode draws the feeding of the crowd to a close and introduces the boat and the trip across the sea. The second episode sets the scene for the walking on the water. The dismissal of the crowd is matter of fact and calm in its atmosphere. The scene in the evening is one of increasing anxiety: Jesus alone on the land; the boat way out on the sea, beaten by the waves. Once again, as in the description of the Syro-Phoenician woman (Mark 7:26), the narrative comment here, "for the wind was against them," explains not only why they were having so much trouble with the waves but also why the storyteller described it with so much intensity. The climax of the setting is then this confidential comment by the storyteller to the listeners which describes the disciples' frightening and lonely journey.

The implication of the setting, "in the fourth watch of the night," is that the disciples spent most of the night trying to get across the lake against the wind. The Romans divided the night watch from 6:00 P.M. to 6:00 A.M. into four three-hour shifts. The "fourth watch" was 3:00 to 6:00 A.M. The atmosphere of this setting is the tone of impending terror typical of ghost stories, the deep darkness of the night when spirits walk among the tombs. Vincent Price is a master of that tone.

And, just as Mark twice described the four friends making a hole in the roof, Matthew builds the episode to a climax of terror by describing the disciples' fear three times. A literal translation is as follows: "They were terrified, saying, 'It is a ghost!' And they cried out from fear." The narrator first names their fear, then shows it by quoting their cry, and concludes with a short, climactic description. This is a storytelling crescendo of terror. And notice that the emphasis is on the inside views of the disciples' feelings of fear. This is an intensive inside view that appeals for equally intensive identification with the disciples. The disciples' fear is connected with the fear of the unknown, which is in turn associated with spirits and ghosts. The word *phantasma* means "an apparition," a seeing of something unknown.

The spirit of Jesus' response is total control and confidence. The episodes juxtapose the extremes of fear and calm, panic and peace. The associations of the divine name in Exodus are built into the story. Jesus relates to the disciples with the same word and attitude with which Yahweh related to Moses. The impact of these words in the story is ambiguous. On the one hand, Jesus' words are comforting. The effect is to draw us as listeners close to him. But the entire episode—his walking on the water, speaking to them while doing it and using the divine name—portrays strange and alien things. As a result, the account also creates a high degree of emotional distance from Jesus. He is clearly a person who is very different from a normal human being. He is radically "other."

Peter responds in the spirit of Jesus' command, "Have no fear." Fearlessly, he asks Jesus to call him to walk on the water. Peter's spirit is the spirit of a child who, without fear, tests the water for the first time. And Jesus' response is equally enthusiastic. I hear this episode as being full of good cheer and high adventure.

The next episode begins on the same note a ringmaster would use in describing a phenomenal feat by the tightrope walking star of the circus. It is a note of wonder and victory: "He did it!" The walking is described from an observer's point of view. But then the narrative perspective shifts. Matthew goes into Peter's head and describes first what Peter sees and then his feeling of fear. The climax of the episode is his cry of panic, its volume, loud, its tone, terror. Again, this is an extreme reversal from the confidence of his request and the success of his walking.

The major question in this story is the tone of Jesus' response. Most interpreters implicitly hear Jesus' tone as being critical, a reproval of Peter. The options are the tone of a critic or a coach. The tone is up close and personal as they stand there on the water together, with Jesus holding Peter up by the arm. And I hear Jesus' words spoken in the tone of a coach, slightly teasing and pointing out Peter's mistake clearly but with smiling disappointment—like a coach who says after a near success, "Ah, why did you lose confidence and blow it? You almost did it!" And the effect is to build confidence in the immediate aftermath of the failure by presence and support.

The story ends in a return to the calm of the story's beginning in the boat and in the appropriate response of the disciples in the boat. Unspoken but implicit is respect for Peter, who did it but couldn't sustain it. That is, the primary appeal of the story is to identify with Peter in his near miss and, from that perspective, to experience Jesus' presence and support as one who is God and has all these terrors under control.

Connections

Connections with biblical stories move in two directions. Often we start with episodes of our own lives and seek connections with biblical stories from that perspective. The experiences of God's self-revelation are approached from within the context of our stories. The other way is to begin with the biblical stories themselves. In this approach, we let God's story establish the context for connection. The story becomes a vessel into which we can pour our own experience. But our experience is then shaped and contained in this broader story.

At the deepest level of the life of the spirit, these connections are made by God. The invitation is then to listen for the links God is seeking to make with us. And in ways that are as infinitely nuanced as the character of God and of each person, God makes those connections with us. God has chosen these stories for a particular and distinctive role in God's relationship with us. To explore our connections with these stories is to pay attention to the movement of God's Spirit within us as we learn, study, internalize, and share these stories.

The invitation is to bring to the story our deepest fears of evil powers beyond our control. These powers are symbolized here by the darkness, the wind, the loneliness of the disciples' night on the boat, and finally by Jesus himself as the unknown spirit walking on the water. What is made clear in this story is that those powers are controlled by Jesus.

The field of experience addressed by the first part of this story is the terrors of the night. A way of discovering your link with this story is then to tell the stories of your most frightening experiences. For me, these stories are connected with lonely cemeteries and empty churches at night, with sailing in sudden storms, and with vicious dogs. For others, they are connected with primary fears of heights or open spaces, of flying or being left alone.

My most vividly frightening experience occurred when I was about ten. My buddy Jim Peffley and I were sledding down in Hardscrabble Park. It was one of those days when shadows scuttled across the snow from the variations in the cloud cover. Although the park was in the middle of town, it was about a half mile wide, with a creek running down through the middle. And it was pretty desolate—lots of woods and scruffy shrubs, water moccasins in parts of the creek, and raccoons in the woods. On a hill across the park was the cemetery. Between the cemetery and where we were sledding, there was a broad field leading down to the creek and across another field to our hill. Usually there were a lot of kids sledding. But, on this particular day, no one else was there—just Jim and me. Now you also need to know that Jim had a powerful imagination, as did I. And he also liked to play tricks on me. Huck Finn and Tom Sawyer had nothing on Peffley and me.

We were having a great time on this slope. There was a little bump in the middle. If we hit it right, our sleds would fly in the air a couple of feet or so. And when we yelled, the sound would echo around the park in a lonely kind of way. Down there in the park we couldn't see anybody else at all. It was a little spooky. But the sledding was so great we didn't care. Still, I remember saying to Peffley, "Man, it sure is quiet down here." And we would stop for a second and listen to the wind and look out across that broad expanse of snow at the shadows on the snow.

We got back up to the top of the hill and were about to make another run when Peffley said, "Hey, Boomer, did you see that? Over there in the cemetery? It looked like something was moving." I looked across the valley. It was more than a quarter of a mile and I didn't see anything except some trees and the tombstones. "Nah, I don't see anything." Peffley said, "Well, it must have just been my imagination. But I'd swear I saw something movin' over there." And we looked again. But there was nothing . . . now.

Peffley's comment changed the atmosphere. The whole place started to look ominous—the trees, the snow—and it seemed to get darker. We kept on sledding, trying to be cheerful and to ignore the gathering gloom. But it just got scarier and scarier. Suddenly, Peffley said, "Look! It's a panther!" I looked and I swear to this day that I saw a big black panther running down through the cemetery, leaping over the fence and across that snow-covered field toward us. We turned around and ran!

Peffley had to take a different route to get to his house. So I took off alone in the other direction. I had to run through the woods for about a hundred yards. I could hear that panther behind me getting closer and closer. I had on my old clumsy boots with metal buckles. And the sled kept banging into my heels. I was terrified! Once I got out of the woods I had to run through a series of back alleys that ran behind the other houses in town to my house, a quarter mile or so. I could feel that panther getting closer and closer, about ready to pounce. Then about a hundred yards from the house, the sled banged into my heels,

100

and I tripped and fell down. As I fell, I knew this was it! I waited for a second to feel the panther's hot breath and his claws in my back. When it didn't come, somewhat to my surprise, I scrambled up, dropped my sled rope, and ran into the house.

I was crying and absolutely panicked. Mom said, "What happened?" Trying to catch my breath, I told her, "Peffley and I saw a panther down in the park. In the cemetery. It was after me." She smiled gently, apparently knowing something about panthers I didn't know. I remember thinking that there weren't panthers in our region of the country. But panthers escape from zoos all the time. She said, "Well, who saw it?" "Peffley saw it first but then . . . It was coming across the field from the cemetery. I saw it." Mom knew my imagination, how gullible I was and susceptible to suggestion. And she also knew Peffley. She smiled again. "Okay, Peffley saw it first. Well, just take off your coat and your boots. How about some hot chocolate?"

Whenever I tell the story of Jesus and Peter walking on the water, I think of the panther and that moment when I fell down and felt it about to leap on my back, my absolute panic, and Mom's smiling calm. The stories are different but the dynamics are similar. And the stories have a similar history. Both are stories that persons told on themselves about a time when they were scared out of their minds by something that turned out to be largely a figment of their frightened imaginations. There the similarity ends. Nevertheless, it helps me to get in touch with the vitality of Matthew's story to tell my story about the panther.

With regard to Peter walking on the water, I remember another incident. Peffley was only indirectly involved in this one. We had regular challenges as to who could do the best tricks on their bikes. My blue and white sixteen-inch Western Flyer wasn't the greatest bike in the world. But it was sturdy and rode pretty steadily. We had been through a lot together, that Western Flyer and I. One day, when I was riding up and down the road outside our house, I was trying various tricks. I could do all of them well: one foot on the handlebars, both feet on the seat and sort of standing up. Peffley was going to be impressed! I would get up some speed coming down a little hill, then I would coast and do my tricks.

It was a little risky. Since cars would come along every once in a while, I had to stay pretty close to the side of the road. And just off the pavement was loose gravel for about two feet between the road and the grass ditch. If you got caught in that gravel, you were in deep trouble.

I came up with a great idea for a trick. It was easy to put my feet up on the handlebars and balance on the seat as long as I held on to the handlebars. Why not let go, guide the bike with my feet and just sit up? Boy, would Peffley be impressed! I practiced the feel of it several times, just holding on very lightly. And then I knew I was ready.

I got up my nerve and some good speed so I could coast and relax. I put my feet up on the handlebars—it felt good! I let go of the handlebars, lightly, and got my balance. Then I leaned back slowly until I was sitting on the seat! No hands! It was like I was flying! Boy, were they going to be impressed. But then I saw a bump coming up and when I moved, the bike started to wobble. All of a sudden I was at least ten feet off the ground. I was losing it! I tried to get my hands back on the handlebars. They were too far! I couldn't make it to the grass. It was so far down to the gravel. I yelled, "Aaaaa!" The gravel came up to meet me and the bike was all over and under me. Crash! Smash!

It was my worst smash-up ever—pants torn, leg all scraped up, arm bloody. And I bent the handlebars on my Western Flyer. That moment of victory which turned into a moment of disaster is indelibly marked in my memory. I know what Peter went through when he first walked on the water and then saw the wind and was scared and began to sink. To remember my story gives me a point of connection with the dynamics of Peter's story.

For Jesus' words, I remember some experiences coaching baseball and soccer and teaching piano. In these ways, my stories are a resource for telling the stories of the Gospels. But also, because of the depth of those stories in my memory, connecting them with the Gospel stories gives them a new context. Several people have spoken in recent years of a "healing of memory." I find that making connections between my story and biblical stories does precisely that. It calls forth memories from deep within myself. Many of them are things I had completely forgotten. And by giving them a new context, it heals my memory. Some of the hurt and terror is taken away, little by little. By reliving my most traumatic experiences in the context of Christ's life, the experiences become a resource rather than something to be repressed. And in workshops, I find that telling them frees people to make their own connections with the stories in ways that are often healing for them.

Telling the Story

The most powerful and potentially redemptive context in which to tell this story is in relation to present experiences of terror and the radical testing of faith. A question that I often ask a group that is exploring this story is "In what way are you now experiencing fears of the unknown or are doing something you have never done before and are afraid you will lose it?" After I have shared that present experience, my partner can tell me the story. No analysis, no suggestions—just active and sympathetic listening and telling the story. Then I, as a listener, am free to explore the connections that emerge from the story's interaction with my story.

There is a story about this story that I would like to share with you. It is told by Mal Bertram, pastor of The Community Church (UCC) in Syosset, New York.

Marie is a white, middle-age woman who in pastoral counseling acknowledged that she was an agoraphobic (fear of spaces). This phobia resulted in the inability to drive, extreme reluctance to leave the confines of her home, and reliance upon tranquilizers. The phobia had serious effects on her social life, requiring deceit and lying as to why she was unable to go places or accept invitations for such common things as a coffee klatch. And it created growing stress on herself and her family.

The pastor suggested the formation of a healing team drawn from a list of persons Marie felt had a depth of faith from which she could draw—not necessarily friends. Six persons were chosen. Discussion of the phobia, its impact on Marie's life, and the introduction of Matthew 14:22-23 (Jesus' walking on the water) followed. The use of space in the story, fear, and the word "courage" were studied, and these elements of the story were used as the basis for personal identification with the story by each team member. The story was learned by all the members. The story quickly became Marie's story.

We agreed that each of the team members would be available on a continual basis as a resource to Marie, in person or by phone, for her to contact when she needed to hear the story. She also was able to tell herself the story. In the course of learning the story, discussion was held around such questions as "When have I been most fearful? perplexed? puzzled? not believing what I was seeing or experiencing?"

While each member of the team related to these questions and to the story, Marie integrated her experiences of fear with each area of discussion.

Slowly Marie began to venture out of the house, drive greater distances, and to reduce her dependence on tranquilizers. She began to challenge her fear with faith. This happened within three months after the group began meeting.

The high point of the healing team's life was a coincidental invitation by the spouse of a healing team member to have a social event on a houseboat. Recognizing that this event could be filled with threat for Marie, he first withdrew the invitation apologetically. But Marie insisted, "I would like to try it." The coincidence of the houseboat, Marie's fear, and the biblical story was readily apparent to everyone. Plans were made for all to arrive at the houseboat for the retelling of the story. After the telling of the story, all ten of us embraced Marie and said to her: "Courage! Don't be afraid! I am with you!" The day was a great success and it ended with a full awareness that Marie had broken the limits imposed by her phobia. She is now 85-90 percent cured of the phobia, rarely uses tranquilizers, and has been able to face life and its challenges as a more whole human being.

The story of Marie's experience was retold widely in the Network of Biblical Storytellers. And Marie's story has had its own life history. The personal narrative that follows is shared by Judy Gorsuch. Judy and I started at Union together and became friends as she dated and then married my first-year roommate, Ken. She and Ken are co-pastors of West End Collegiate Church on the upper West Side of Manhattan.

When I was involved in a continuing education course at Union Theological Seminary in New York, I met Peg Eddy who told me about the work of the Network of Biblical Storytellers, including the story of Marie and her healing. Peg did not tell me the source of Marie's story, but I found all of it very interesting and tucked the information away in my mind for further consideration sometime.

Several months later on a very hot Sunday in July, I was liturgist for morning worship and was sitting in a large chair on the dais enjoying the sermon. The room which was being used as a temporary sanctuary because of a recent fire at our church was extremely hot and crowded that day, and I was robed in heavy vestments with long sleeves and a high collar. Suddenly I felt very hot and then faint. I was horrified at the thought of disrupting worship by fainting flat out during the sermon. I struggled to control my breathing and soon I was all right. I thought no more about it.

The next Sunday, however, sitting in the same chair during worship, the sensation of fainting returned, perhaps by association. Once again I struggled to regain control and did, but it was the same the next Sunday and the next. Soon I was beginning to be anxious about Sunday worship, not only on Sunday mornings but also for days ahead. "This is silly," I thought, "I should be able to control this," but I could not and realized that I was beginning to develop a phobic fear of fainting in worship!

Then I remembered the story that Peg had told me about Marie. I memorized the story of Jesus walking on the water in Matthew, concentrating especially on the phrase "Take heart, it is I; have no fear." On Sundays after that, if fear of fainting began to overtake me, I repeated these words to myself and pictured Jesus reaching out to me, keeping me from sinking into anxiety. Knowing the story behind the words enabled me to feel the power of Jesus' strength and presence. Gradually over several months the fear of fainting subsided, and I was not longer plagued with anxious feelings during worship.

Almost a whole year later, I went to a conference of the Network of Biblical Storytellers in Maine and attended there a workshop led by Mal Bertram, whom I had never met. Mal started to talk about the use of biblical storytelling in pastoral work and told the story of one of his parishioners named Marie. Suddenly I realized that this was the man who, along with members of his congregation, had helped me to be healed without their ever knowing it. When the workshop was over, I told Mal how he had helped me, unbeknownst to him. We marveled at how the story had been spread and the work it had accomplished.

The Gospel as Storytelling in Pastoral Care

In these stories, the potential gift of biblical storytelling in the ministry of counseling and pastoral care can be seen. When the spiritual energy of a story from the tradition of Israel connects with the spiritual needs of a person, profound new perspectives can emerge. God can be present in unique ways through these stories for persons who are afflicted.

In particular, the stories can help to change the feeling that affliction is in some sense caused by God. It is difficult to draw that conclusion unambiguously when one is remembering the stories of God's love and concern.

The stories seem to have the most appropriate meaning when told by persons who are part of a support network. Somehow the telling of personal stories about how the stories have had meaning for others gives them a context. A problem for many people is an assumption that telling or listening to the stories implies a belief that the stories are somehow magical formulas, or that you expect the same thing will happen to the person as happens in the story. Relating how others have experienced the stories provides a framework of experience that is broader and gives permission for people to listen to the stories in a variety of ways. When left free to listen, persons often make connections with the story that are surprising as well as fully appropriate. No counselor could ever foresee the helpful connections that sometimes emerge.

The role of the gospel as storytelling in counseling and pastoral care has its source in the tradition of spiritual direction. Particularly in the Ignatian tradition, meditating on the stories of Jesus' life, death, and resurrection is a primary resource for hearing God's voice in the interior intimacy of the spirit. A hope is that opening ourselves to the recovery of the gospel as storytelling may provide a new context in which we can perceive and receive more fully the love of God that is there for us as a free gift.

6

A SYRO-PHOENICIAN WOMAN

(Mark 7:24-30)

This story is about the action of God in establishing peace and justice in the midst of the enmities that develop between human groups. Jesus' action in relation to the Syro-Phoenician woman makes it clear that the source of peace and reconciliation is an honest and just crossing of the boundaries that separate enemies. The story creates a new relationship between enemies. The way of the Messiah is to make peace between enemies. One way to learn the ways of peace is to learn the stories of God's actions for peace and justice. Telling the stories of God opens a new range of possibilities for Christian social action.

The Story

And from there he arose and went away to the region of
   Tyre and Sidon.
And he entered a house and wanted no one to know.
Yet he could not be hid.

☆　☆　☆　☆　☆

But immediately a woman, whose little daughter was
   possessed by an unclean spirit, heard of him, and
   came and fell down at his feet.

Now the woman was a Greek, a Syrophoenician by birth.
And she begged him to cast the demon out of her
daughter.

☆ ☆ ☆ ☆ ☆

And he said to her, "Let the children first be fed.
For it is not right to take the children's bread and throw it
to the dogs."
But she answered him, "Yes, Lord; yet even the dogs
under the table eat the children's crumbs."

☆ ☆ ☆ ☆ ☆

And he said to her, "For this saying you may go your way.
The demon has left your daughter."
And she went home, and found the child lying in bed, and
the demon gone.

Learning the Story

The four episodes of the story have a typical healing-story
structure: setting, the woman and her request, direct discourse
between Jesus and the woman, the pronouncement, and
confirmation of the healing.

Verbal Threads

"The demon out of her daughter." This is the most important
verbal thread in the story. The woman's request at the end of
the second episode is that he "cast the demon out of her
daughter" (vs. 26). The last two sentences of the final episode
reiterate the theme but with a new verb, "left" *(ekselaluthen)*;
Jesus says, "the demon has left your daughter" (vs. 29) and
(literal translation) "the woman goes home, finds her daughter
in bed, and the demon had left" (vs. 30).

"The dogs." This phrase is the verbal yarn that weaves
together Jesus' statement and the woman's response (vss.
27-28). The woman's statement picks up and reweaves Jesus'
words in an artful way. A literal translation of the words is as
follows:

Jesus—"Allow first to be fed the children [*tekna*]. For it is
  not right to take the bread of the children and throw
  it to the dogs" (vs. 27).
Woman—"Yes sir, and the dogs under the table eat from
  the crumbs of the kids [*paidion*]" (vs. 28).

We do not know the precise connotations of the two different
words for children used here by Jesus and the woman. The
woman's word *(paidion)* is connected in Mark with the story of
the healing of Jairus's (a synagogue elder) daughter (5:21-23,
35-43), Jesus' discourse on service to children as service to him
(9:36-37), and the story of Jesus blessing the children
(10:13-16). As a result, her statement is positively related to
prominent themes in Jesus' teaching and actions throughout
Mark's narrative. The translation "kids" may catch some of the
affection for children that the word implies.

Scenes

Scene 1. Wide pan shot of Jesus' trip to Tyre, Jesus entering a
house secretly, and the rumor spreading among the people of
the town.

Scene 2. Wide shot of the Syro-Phoenician woman falling at
his feet and begging him to help her daughter.

Scene 3. Close-up of the discussion between Jesus and the
woman about the dogs.

Scene 4. Close-up of Jesus' words and pan back to the woman
going home and finding the daughter in bed and the demon
gone.

Listening to the Story

Our goal is to hear the depth of the story's impact in its
original context.

Tyre and Sidon were coastal cities in what is now Lebanon.
The fact that they were primary targets of the Israeli invasion of
Lebanon is indicative of their relationship to the community of
Israel then as well as now. From the days of Jezebel to the
present, these cities have been the enemies of Israel. Jesus' trip

109

was then a trip into enemy territory. The only earlier mention of Tyre and Sidon in Mark is a description of the crowds who came to hear and be healed by Jesus (3:8). This probably indicates that the narrator presented this trip in a relatively objective rather than a negative or hostile manner.

The episode about the woman's action, however, was probably presented with an attitude of incredulousness and amazement. For a Syro-Phoenician woman to make this request, in the context of the relationships between Syrians and Israelites, was almost unprecedented. The only precedent in the tradition of Israel for such a request from an enemy is the story of Naaman, the general of the Syrian army, who traveled to Israel to ask Elisha to cure his leprosy (II Kings 5). Relationships between Israelites and Syrians in the intervening period since mid-ninth century B.C. had certainly not improved. The question raised by her action is, why would she do such a thing? What is the spirit of this plea? The possibilities are either arrogance or its exact opposite, an extreme humility. In the context of first-century politics, the general assumption of Jewish listeners would be that a Syro-Phoenician woman would only make such a request out of arrogance.

That assumption was based on recent memory. One of the most vivid narrative memories in the tradition of Israel in Jesus' period was the persecution of Jews by Antiochus Epiphanes and specifically, the report of his public trials recorded in II Maccabees 6 and 7. The most poignant story is the martyrdom of seven brothers and their mother, who were arrested and publicly tortured to death by Antiochus because they wouldn't eat pork (II Macc. 7). I would suggest that you read the story, perhaps even aloud, as a way of hearing the context of Mark's narrative in the first century.

It happened also that seven brothers and their mother were arrested and were being compelled by the king, under torture with whips and cords, to partake of unlawful swine's flesh. One of them, acting as their spokesman, said, "What do you intend to ask and learn from us? For we are ready to die rather than transgress the laws of our fathers."

The king fell into a rage, and gave orders that pans and caldrons be heated. These were heated immediately, and he commanded that the tongue of their spokesman be cut out and that they scalp him and cut off his hands and feet, while the rest of the brothers and the mother looked on. When he was utterly helpless, the king ordered them to take him to the fire, still breathing, and to fry him in a pan. The smoke from the pan spread widely, but the brothers and their mother encouraged one another to die nobly, saying, "The Lord God is watching over us and in truth has compassion on us, as Moses declared in his song which bore witness against the people to their faces, when he said, 'And he will have compassion on his servants.' "

After the first brother had died in this way, they brought forward the second for their sport. They tore off the skin of his head with the hair, and asked him, "Will you eat rather than have your body punished limb by limb?" He replied in the language of his fathers, and said to them, "No." Therefore he in turn underwent tortures as the first brother had done. And when he was at his last breath, he said, "You accursed wretch, you dismiss us from this present life, but the King of the universe will raise us up to an everlasting renewal of life, because we have died for his laws."

After him, the third was the victim of their sport. When it was demanded he quickly put out his tongue and courageously stretched forth his hands, and said nobly, "I got these from Heaven, and because of his laws I disdain them, and from him I hope to get them back again." As a result, the king himself and those with him were astonished at the young man's spirit, for he regarded his sufferings as nothing.

When he too had died, they maltreated and tortured the fourth in the same way. And when he was near death, he said, "One cannot but choose to die at the hands of men and to cherish the hope that God gives of being raised again by him. But for you there will be no resurrection to life!"

Next they brought forward the fifth and maltreated him. But he looked at the king, and said, "Because you have authority among men, mortal though you are, you do what you please. But do not think that God has forsaken our people. Keep on, and see how his mighty power will torture you and your descendants!"

After him they brought forward the sixth. And when he was about to die, he said, "Do not deceive yourself in vain. For we are suffering these things on our own account, because of our sins against our own God. Therefore astounding things have happened. But do not think that you will go unpunished for having tried to fight against God!"

The mother was especially admirable and worthy of honorable memory. Though she saw her seven sons perish within a single day, she bore it with good courage because of her hope in the Lord. She encouraged each of them in the language of their fathers. Filled with a noble spirit, she fired her woman's reasoning with a man's courage, and said to them, "I do not know how you came into being in my womb. It was not I who gave you life and breath, nor I who set in order the elements within each of you. Therefore the Creator of the world, who shaped the beginning of man and devised the origin of all things, will in his mercy give life and breath back to you again, since you now forget yourselves for the sake of his laws."

Antiochus felt that he was being treated with contempt, and he was suspicious of her reproachful tone. The youngest brother being still alive, Antiochus not only appealed to him in words, but promised with oaths that he would make him rich and enviable if he would turn from the ways of his fathers, and that he would take him for his friend and entrust him with public affairs. Since the young man would not listen to him at all, the king called the mother to him and urged her to advise the youth to save himself. After much urging on his part she undertook to persuade her son. But, leaning close to him, she spoke in their native tongue as follows, deriding the cruel tyrant: "My son, have pity on me. I carried you nine months in my womb, and nursed you for three years, and have reared you and brought you up to this point in your life, and have taken care of you. I beseech you, my child, to look at the heaven and the earth and see everything that is in them, and recognize that God did not make them out of things that existed. Thus also mankind comes into being. Do not fear this butcher, but prove worthy of your brothers. Accept death, so that in God's mercy I may get you back again with your brothers."

While she was still speaking, the young man said, "What are you waiting for? I will not obey the king's command, but I obey the command of the law that was given to our fathers through Moses. But you, who have contrived all sorts of evil against the Hebrews, will certainly not escape the hands of God. For we are suffering because of our own sins. And if our living Lord is angry for a little while, to rebuke and discipline us, he will again be reconciled with his own servants. But you, unholy wretch, you most defiled of all men, do not be elated in vain and puffed up by uncertain hopes, when you raise your hand against the children of heaven. You have not yet escaped the judgment of the almighty, all-seeing God. For our brothers after enduring a brief suffering have drunk of everflowing life under God's covenant; but you, by the judgment of God, will receive just punishment for your arrogance. I, like my brothers, give up body and life for the laws of our fathers, appealing to God to show mercy soon to our nation and by afflictions and plagues to make you confess that he alone is God, and through me and my brothers to bring to an end the wrath of the Almighty which has justly fallen on our whole nation."

The king fell into a rage, and handled him worse than the others, being exasperated at his scorn. So he died in his integrity, putting his whole trust in the Lord. Last of all, the mother died, after her sons.

Let this be enough, then, about the eating of sacrifices and the extreme tortures. (RSV Apocrypha)

This event probably took place in approximately 169 B.C. The stories of II Maccabees 6 and 7 were early Jewish martyr stories. The stories themselves were retold frequently, as is reflected in IV Maccabees, in which the principal subject is a more elaborate retelling of the story of the mother and her seven boys. The memories were, therefore, fresh and current for Mark and his listeners.

When seen against the background of this Jewish mother's intercessions for her seven sons, this Gentile woman's request on behalf of her daughter is shocking. The evidence that Mark reported the woman's request as a potential scandal is the position of his explanation of the woman's identity ("Now the woman was a Greek"—vs. 26). This narrative comment follows his description that the woman came in and fell at Jesus' feet. The function of these comments to the audience is to explain something surprising or puzzling in the previous statement. The fact that a woman whose daughter had an unclean spirit came and fell at Jesus' feet is no surprise. Men and women have been doing that throughout the story. The most graphic instance is the synagogue elder, Jairus, who fell at Jesus' feet and asked Jesus to heal his daughter (5:22). The comment, therefore, explained why the narrator reported her action with incredulousness and disbelief. The climax of the episode is then that *she,* a Gentile, asked him, a Jew, to cast the demon out of her daughter. In the context of the relationship between their nations, such a request was incredible.

The narrative comment is one indication that the telling of this story was shaped by Jewish norms. Another is the issue of the cleanliness laws. In Mark, this story follows Jesus' dispute with the Pharisees about the cleanliness laws in regard to food (7:1-23). Jesus' reinterpretation of the cleanliness laws is that what makes persons unclean is not the food they eat or whether they have washed their hands. What makes persons unclean is what comes out of their hearts. This reinterpretation of the cleanliness laws is of particular importance in relation to Gentiles like this woman. The system of food laws was one of the social structures that separated Jews from Gentiles. As is reflected in the story of Antiochus Epiphanes, the eating of pork was a battle line between Jews and Gentiles. Jews did not eat with Gentiles because they would be made unclean by the food. To attack the cleanliness laws was to attack the social structures that kept Israelites separated from their Gentile enemies. In this story, Jesus tests the spirit of this Gentile woman. He determines what is in her heart.

But the manner of Jesus' test is anything but gentle. The storytelling issue is how Jesus' words about the bread and the dogs were spoken. And the evidence is clear that Jesus' words were confrontational and insulting. The images associated with throwing bread to the dogs are those of the garbage dump and the arena where people were thrown to the dogs. The phrases of Psalm 22 are indicative:

> Many bulls surround me,
> strong bulls of Bashan surround me;
> Roaring lions tearing their prey
> open their mouths wide against me
> . . . .
> Dogs have surrounded me;
> a band of evil men encircled me,
> . . . .
> Deliver my life from the sword,
> my precious life from the power of the dogs.
> Rescue me from the mouth of the lions,
> save me from the horns of the wild oxen.
>
> (vss. 12-13, 16, 20-21 NIV)

Packs of wild dogs were vicious predators in the ancient world, and, as is indicated by the associations in Psalm 22, they were generally feared and hated.

At the heart of the issue between Jesus and the woman is whether she will accept the insult of being called a dog. How the story was heard depends on the justice of Jesus' insult. In the context of what Syrians had done to Jews, the term was both just and appropriate. And, in the context of the story, the narrator assumes that the listeners will share this judgment.

Surprisingly, the woman accepts Jesus' description of her as a dog. It is an incredible response in the context of the social and political relationships of Jesus' day. But she also reinterprets

Jesus' metaphor and appeals to a growing pattern of domestication of dogs as house pets. This redefinition of herself as a house pet is the linguistic dimension of her appeal for a new relationship to the blessings of the kingdom of God.

Her statement reveals what is in her heart. She has set aside all prideful assumptions of superiority and has made herself vulnerable for the sake of her daughter. Her words make clear that her spirit is a spirit of extraordinary humility, the exact opposite of arrogance. She too has crossed the boundaries between enemies. She has shown courage and a perseverant faith. Her action is like that of the woman with a flow of blood (Mark 5:25-34) who risked further social ostracism and the possibility of Jesus' hostility out of a determined faith. This story's greatest surprise is that such faith would be found in a Gentile.

The pause that separates her appeal from Jesus' concluding response is the story's answer to the question of whether Jesus knew what he was going to do beforehand. In the story, the pause is the time when the suspense rises, Jesus ponders and perhaps quietly smiles, and then speaks. No one could have foreseen the woman's response to his insult. Likewise, no one in the telling of the story can know how Jesus will respond. The silence even implies the possibility that the woman's response taught Jesus something about Gentiles. The norm of judgment that provides the context for Jesus' evaluation of her statement is his own redefinition of cleanliness. And what comes out of the woman's heart is *clean*.

The appeal of the story is to respond to Jesus' action as a sign of the kingdom of God rather than as collusion with the enemy. The help that is given to the woman is in response to her acceptance of Jesus' testing. His extension of the gifts of peace is based, therefore, on the establishment of justice in their communal relationship. Just as Mark invites the listeners to share the joy of Jairus and his wife when they saw their daughter get up and walk around the room, so also this story invites the listeners to share the joy implicit in this Gentile woman's discovery of her daughter in bed and the demon *gone!*

Connections

The primary connection between this story and our experience is relationships with enemies. Who is the enemy? The enemy is a role, a pattern of relationship, into which many persons are cast. A parent, a child, or a spouse can become an enemy, as can a fellow worker, a boss, or a teacher/professor. But we primarily define our enemies in relation to other groups; another nation, religion, race, or ethnic group. Many human groups are in part defined by having a common enemy. And those enemies may change with time. Thus, in American history the enemies of longest standing have been England and then Germany, both of whom are now among the nation's closest allies. The Soviet Union and "communism" have taken their place as the national enemies. In the story of virtually every person and group, the enemies can be identified.

In order to connect with this story, therefore, the first question is, who are your enemies? I would suggest that you make an enemies list. And, as you make the list, remember those specific events of conflict and, if they are present, of reconciliation with those persons or groups. A recommendation is that you not only list those persons or groups whom you feel to be your enemies but also those who are the enemies of the groups with whom you are identified simply because of who you are. Thus, as a white, male, middle-class, liberal Protestant, Christian American, there are groups who regard me and the groups with which I am identified as enemies. And whether or not I feel enmity toward those groups, the fact is that in some sense they are my enemies.

One way of understanding enmity is in relation to boundaries. Persons and groups that are alienated from each other build up boundaries against their enemies. These boundaries take many different forms: national boundaries, turf lines, patterns of social life, and eating habits. A next step in exploring the connections with this story is to identify the boundaries that operate in your personal and social context that keep you separated from your enemies.

For example, in the United States, the structures for the separation or segregation of black and white Americans are extremely complex. In the aftermath of the civil rights movement, the separation of racial groups at public facilities such as buses, restaurants, restrooms, and swimming pools has been largely eliminated. Efforts have been made to eliminate the separations in schools, housing, and work. But I recognize that there are many structures in every aspect of my life that tend to separate me as a white man from persons who are black.

The enemies list is a resource for connecting with the dynamics of this story. When have you had an explicit confrontation with an enemy that ended in some kind of reconciliation or giving between you? How did you cope with the fact of your enmity with each other? The suggestion would be that you remember that story and tell it to yourself or to someone else. The emotions and dynamics of that encounter may be a resource for helping you to find a way of presenting this story of Jesus and the Syro-Phoenician woman.

Another way of connecting with the story that has proven to be helpful for some people has been a kind of story theater. It is a form of mutual storytelling in which two people tell the story to each other as persons within the story. In this story, one person would tell Jesus' parts of the story and the other the woman's parts:

The setting (episode 1)—Jesus, trying to hide
The woman (episode 2)—woman, falling at Jesus' feet
Jesus' words (episode 3, sentences 1, 2)—Jesus
The woman's response (episode 3, sentence 3)—the woman
Jesus' blessing and words of healing (episode 4, sentences 1, 2)—Jesus
The confirmation of the healing (episode 4, sentence 3)—the woman

In this exploration, as the story is told, each person acts out the relationship in order to discover the feelings and dynamics of the encounter. And, after doing it one way, the roles are exchanged and each person tells the other part of the story. Talking about the feelings that are generated by telling the story is often helpful. How does it feel to be the woman? Jesus? Finally, the whole story is told by each person so that the integrity of the story is preserved.

The connection that helps me understand this story happened during my first year in New York. For my field work at Union, I was hired as organist and choirmaster at Chambers Memorial Baptist Church in East Harlem, one of New York's ghetto communities. Chambers was a small American Baptist urban mission congregation. Not only had I never been in New York before, I had never been in a black community before.

It was the fall of 1962, the height of the civil rights movement. As I rode back across 125th Street on Sunday afternoons, I remember seeing large gatherings around Malcolm X, who was reputed to be preaching hatred of whites. I was often the only white man on the bus. Although no one was ever directly hostile to me, I felt like I was an enemy. And the more I learned about the ongoing effects of white racism, the more appropriate it became.

The choir was a small group of men and women who loved to sing. I was very nervous and unsure of myself. I now know how kind they were to me. But things weren't going very well. After church one autumn Sunday, Thelma Cockerham invited me to come to dinner that Wednesday night at her house next door to the church. I will never know what happened. I had not yet learned to write things down. And, with the combination of Union and Chambers, I was in more or less total cultural shock. But, for whatever reason, the next Sunday Thelma approached me with fire in her eyes: "Where were you on Wednesday night?" Only then did I remember. I had forgotten! To say "I forgot" had been a rather familiar excuse for me in high school. But, in this context, it was totally inappropriate. There was nothing to say except: "I am sorry. Forgive me." She said: "I fixed you a turkey dinner with all the trimmings. And you couldn't even remember." As my fellow field work students pointed out to me, this was not only unforgivable, it was also *stupid*, because Thelma was a great cook and her turkey dinners were legendary.

Thelma never forgot, nor did I. There was no cheap grace. It was a primal consciousness-raising experience for me about myself as a white man. Nervousness or fear was absolutely irrelevant. The only thing that counted was faithfulness and remembering. But the incredible fact was that during that year I found myself loved by the people of that church, and particularly by Thelma. Experiencing this kind of love, tough love which cuts across the boundaries that separate people, convinced me that I wanted to become an ordained minister. That is the kind of love Jesus shared with the Syro-Phoenician woman and her daughter.

Telling the Story

If one were to make a list of Jesus' enemies in the first century—sinners, various unclean persons, tax collectors, Gentiles, scribes, Pharisees—it would be striking how many of the stories of his ministry involve encounters in which Jesus took the initiative to cross the boundaries that separated him from his enemies. The invitation of the story tradition is then to tell and hear these stories in relation to the boundaries that separate us from our enemies. The stories reveal the character of God who loves God's enemies. And God steadily works to bring about reconciliation with those who are separated from God and between persons and groups who are separated from each other. When heard in relation to our enmities, the story may shed light on possible ways in which God is at work to bring about reconciliation and peace.

In a group, a helpful way to tell and hear the story is then to share a present experience of enmity and alienation. It is good to share in relation to both personal and communal enemies. One way of discovering those boundaries is to ask, who are my deepest enemies now? Who is the person or group from which I [we] are most profoundly alienated? And if my friend has shared this with me, I will tell the story of Jesus and the Syro-Phoenician woman to my friend to see what the story might reveal. And after sharing what, if anything, the story meant as we heard it, we will switch. I will describe my present experience of enmity, and my friend will tell me the story. It is also possible for a group to identify their enemies and for one person to tell the story to the group. In some form, however, it is helpful for each person to have the opportunity to talk about what the story meant to them as they heard it.

I remember my first experience of hearing this story for myself. It was during a series on storytelling and peacemaking at a small church outside Dayton. We learned the story and explored its meaning in its original context. When the time came to listen to and tell the story in relation to our present experience, my partner was an older woman. I shared with her that my deepest concern was the enmity between the peoples of the Soviet Union and the United States. When she told me the story, it was immediately clear what needed to be done. We, as the Network of Biblical Storytellers, needed to organize a storytelling trip to the Soviet Union and try to establish an ongoing storytelling network with families, churches, and storytelling groups there.

As a direct result of that storytelling experience, a storytelling trip is presently being organized to coincide with the millennial anniversary of the establishment of Christianity in Russia, in the summer of 1988. Our hope is to tell stories—biblical, American folk tales, and personal stories about peace—and to invite persons there to share stories with us. Our hope is that this will be the first step in establishing a new pattern of relationships between persons in our two countries.

Storytelling and Peacemaking

The historian Karl Popper has made an interesting observation about the shaping of history. He said, "The making of history has been shaped from the top down with one exception, Jesus of Nazareth and his followers who made history from the bottom up." To whatever degree this is true, a primary factor in the impact of Jesus' movement has been the storytelling of his followers. In the first centuries of the church, Jewish Christians aggressively told the stories of Jesus to those from whom they were separated: Romans, Greeks, slaves, the rich, and soldiers. Their mission of telling the stories of good news was a foundation stone for the new patterns of relationship that were established in the church and in Roman society.

The simple suggestion that emerges from this realization is that telling the stories of God's peace may have a significant role to play in peacemaking now. To listen to and learn the stories of our enemies and make them our own is one step. To listen for ways in which to tell the stories of the actions of God in relation to our enemies' alienation from us is another. And ways may emerge that will enable our enemies to tell us the stories of the Gospels in the context of their experience. Approaching the gospel as storytelling has been and may again be a principal resource for making history from the bottom up.

7

BARTIMAEUS

(Mark 10:46-52)

The story of Bartimaeus is an experience of the healing power of faith that leads to discipleship. It begins in identification with the humiliation of a blind beggar sitting in the dust. It ends with his sight restored as he follows Jesus on the way up to Jerusalem. In a unique way, this story concretizes the power of the faith of persons who are oppressed by physical or mental handicaps, patriarchal social structures, racial discrimination, and economic systems over which they have no control. It is an invitation to allow our own personal and communal humiliation to be seen in the context of Bartimaeus's faith in Jesus as the Christ.

The Story

And they came to Jericho.
And as he was leaving Jericho with his disciples and a
    great multitude, Bartimaeus, a blind beggar, the son
    of Timaeus, was sitting by the roadside.

☆   ☆   ☆   ☆   ☆

And when he heard that it was Jesus of Nazareth, he
    began to cry out and say, "Jesus, Son of David, have
    mercy on me!"
And many rebuked him, telling him to shut up.

☆ ☆ ☆ ☆ ☆

But he cried out all the more, "Son of David, have mercy
    on me!"
And Jesus stopped and said, "Call him."

☆ ☆ ☆ ☆ ☆

And they called the blind man, saying to him, "Take
    heart; rise, he is calling you."
And throwing off his mantle he sprang up and came to
    Jesus.

☆ ☆ ☆ ☆ ☆

And Jesus said to him, "What do you want me to do for
    you?"
And the blind man said to him, "Master, let me receive
    my sight."

☆ ☆ ☆ ☆ ☆

And Jesus said to him, "Go your way; your faith has made
    you well."
And immediately he received his sight and followed him
    on the way.

Learning the Story

Verbal Threads

"**Jericho.**" The first episode is tied together by Jericho: "He
came to Jericho"/"as he was leaving Jericho" (vs. 46).

"**Cried out . . . 'Son of David, have mercy on me.' **" The
first sentences in the episodes of Bartimaeus's crying out for
Jesus have this extensive verbal thread (vss. 47-48).

"Call." Jesus' calling Bartimaeus is linked together by that key word. A literal translation is "Jesus said, 'Call him.' *They called* the blind man saying, "Take heart, get up, *he is calling you*" (vs. 49).

"Receive sight"/"see again." The last sentences of the final episodes are linked by this verbal thread, which is more accurately translated: "that I might see again"/"immediately he could see again" (vss. 51-52).

The first two episodes have a typical ABAC episodic structure in which the first sentences are in synonymous parallelism and the last are in antithetical parallelism. That is, Bartimaeus cries, the crowd tells him to shut up, Bartimaeus cries again louder, and Jesus says, "Call him."

Also notice the manner in which the beginning and ending of the story are linked together by the phrase "the way." The first episode ends with Bartimaeus sitting "by the roadside [way]" begging; the story ends with Bartimaeus following him "on the way" (vss. 46, 52). It is a marvelously concise encapsulation of the transformation of Bartimaeus's life.

This story is easy to learn because of the clarity and simplicity of its structure: setting, first cry, second cry, Jesus' call, Jesus' question and Bartimaeus's answer, the healing. Once the structure is recognized and the verbal threads are recognized, remembering the story is simply a matter of rethinking the structure and its linkages.

Listening to the Story

The story's opening establishes the depth of Bartimaeus's shame by a series of implicit contrasts to pride and glory. The first association with glory in the story is Jericho itself. The foremost associations of Jericho in the tradition of Israel are with the glory of Joshua's victory "when the walls came tumbling down." Jericho is one of the oldest continuously inhabited cities in the world, having been occupied at least since 3000 B.C. and perhaps much earlier.

The introduction of Bartimaeus's name calls further attention to his shame. The sentence has an unusual word order, literally, "the son of Timaeus, Bartimaeus, a blind man, was sitting beside the way begging." Usually an explanation of a name such as "the son of Timaeus" would follow rather than precede the name, for example, "Rabboni (which means 'Teacher')" (John 20:16). The unusual order calls attention to the meaning of Bartimaeus's name. "Timaeus" is based on the Greek word *tima,* which means "honor, reverence"; the name means "one who is honored, revered." *Bar* means "son" in Aramaic; hence, Bartimaeus is "a son of honor." This twice reiterated emphasis on his "honor" is immediately connected with his present condition, "a blind man, sitting beside the road begging." Another dimension of this poignant contrast between honor and shame is implicit in Bartimaeus's request to Jesus (vs. 51). The word Bartimaeus uses *(anablepo)* literally means "to see again," with the implication that once he could see but now he is blind. Thus, the story opens and closes with a highly sympathetic description of Bartimaeus.

His cry is introduced by an inside view, "When he heard that it was Jesus of Nazareth . . ." (vs. 47). The narrator takes us inside Bartimaeus's head and the darkness of his blindness as he hears the cries of Jesus' name being called out by the crowd. This creates a close identification with Bartimaeus.

Bartimaeus's name for Jesus is highly controversial. "Son of David" (vss. 47-48) has never been used as a title for Jesus earlier in the Gospel narrative. The title is associated with the Messiah, who would, as a legitimate heir in the royal succession, restore the Davidic monarchy and the glory of David's kingdom. The phrase "have mercy" is taken directly from the Psalms and is usually translated "be gracious" in the RSV (e.g., Pss. 6:2; 9:13; 30:10; 41:4; 86:3). Bartimaeus's second cry is even louder and more intense than the first.

The crowd's response is first to rebuke and then to encourage him (vss. 48-49). The implication of the rebuke is that they were ashamed of his crying out. But they quickly take their cue from Jesus and change their attitude toward Bartimaeus.

The atmosphere of Bartimaeus's response to Jesus' call is pure enthusiasm (vs. 50). The gestures are built into the story: throwing off the mantle, leaping up and coming to Jesus.

Jesus' question—"What do you want me to do for you?"—to Bartimaeus is connected with the tradition of relationships between prophets and their disciples. Tracing this verbal thread back in time, it leads first to Jesus' identical question to James and John in the immediately preceding story. The account is as follows:

And James and John, the sons of Zebedee, came forward to him, and said to him, "Teacher, we want you to do for us whatever we ask of you." And he said to them, "What do you want me to do for you?" And they said to him, "Grant us to sit, one at your right hand and one at your left, in your glory." (Mark 10:35-37)

Their request is not granted. Instead, Jesus as a prophet instructs them about the limits of his own power. Furthermore, the other disciples' anger requires Jesus to give them a lesson in service.

This question is, however, not original with Jesus. In II Kings, when Elijah is about to be taken up into heaven, Elijah and Elisha cross the Jordan on dry land:

When they had crossed, Elijah said to Elisha, "Ask what I shall do for you, before I am taken from you." And Elisha said, "I pray you, let me inherit a double share of your spirit." And he said, "You have asked a hard thing; yet, if you see me as I am being taken from you, it shall be so for you; but if you do not see me, it shall not be so." (II Kings 2:9-10)

Elijah is taken up into heaven; Elisha sees him and picks up the mantle of Elijah. He strikes the water with the mantle and the waters part. This sign confirms that Elisha has received Elijah's spirit and power.

This tradition clarifies the seriousness of the question in the Bartimaeus story. Prophets ask this question of their disciples when they are about to be taken away from them. And the issue is the transferral of power. In contrast to the self-initiated request of James and John for power that is not granted, Bartimaeus's request is granted. Bartimaeus and his mantle are thereby associated with a distinguished stream of prophetic tradition.

Jesus' response to Bartimaeus's request is also distinctive in the healing narrative tradition. Jesus does nothing: no healing words, no laying on of hands. A literal translation of Jesus' words to the blind man is "Go. Your faith has saved you." The verb is an imperative. It is usually translated "go your way" and is presented as Jesus' command to Bartimaeus to go and live his life in freedom from his blindness. The other possibility is that it means "Go on, see" and refers back to his request for sight. In this interpretation, the command is a response to Bartimaeus's request, which refers back to the power of his own faith. To paraphrase, "Why do you ask me to heal you? Go on, your faith has already saved you." In this telling, Jesus' response is a word of affirmation and encouragement in which he gives permission for Bartimaeus to act on the power implicit in his own faith. This motif occurs in earlier healing stories of Mark (the paralytic, 2:5; the woman with a flow of blood, 5:34, 36; see also 6:6; 9:23). The most direct connection is to the story of the woman. She falls at his feet in fear and trembling and tells him the whole story of what has happened (5:33). The implied sources of her fear are both the possibility of public exposure of her shame and the assumption that Jesus will be furious at her for making him unclean by her secret touch. Jesus' response is then surprising and overwhelmingly affirmative of the woman's own role in her healing: "Daughter, your faith has saved you. Go in peace and be healed permanently of your disease" (5:34). Jesus' word to Bartimaeus has the same character. It is an affirmation of his courage and faith and is an encouragement to allow that faith to be fully lived out.

The culmination of the story is Bartimaeus's receiving his sight and following Jesus on the way. The ending is a celebration of victory. The shortness of the sentence is a sign that the narrator made this a climactic moment, with full emphasis on the change in Bartimaeus's status. He has gone from being a blind beggar to being a follower of the Messiah, the son of David.

Connections

The situations from your own experience that may provide vital connections with this story are relatively easy to identify:

primary experiences of humiliation and shame, of being in the dust; crying out for help; both hearing and encouraging someone who needs help; experiences of the dawning of hope in the midst of desperation; conversations in which few words are spoken but the rest of your life is on the line. The most striking element of this story is Bartimaeus's cry of faith. Therefore, finding the link to the integrity and authenticity of Bartimaeus's crying out is the key to making this story come alive.

But, in addition to exploring this on your own, there are ways of exploring this story in a group that can make it a resource for the faith of not only individuals but also communities. In his book *Transforming Bible Study,* Walter Wink has outlined a method of Bible study called communal exegesis. In this process, the role of the leader is to ask questions that will lead a group into exploring a biblical text themselves. These questions move naturally from the context and meaning of biblical materials in their own historical context to their meaning now. This approach to biblical study has proven to be highly generative for the transformation of persons and local churches.

In a recent doctor of ministry demonstration project, Margaret Eddy has explored the integration of communal exegesis with a storytelling approach to biblical narratives. The group with whom she worked is called the East Harlem Healing Community. It is an ecumenical group of black, Hispanic, and white women and men who have actively explored the biblical storytelling tradition as a resource for personal and communal healing and reconciliation. Her project was focused on the story of Bartimaeus and the development of a series of storytelling experiences around this story.

Preparing to lead a group in communal exegesis begins with the careful identification of a series of questions that are both focused and open-ended. The role of the leader is to guide the group into an exploration of these questions without giving "the answers." In the process, the group discovers connections between the story and their own experience that could never emerge without the openness created by the group's own exploration.

The following questions were developed by Margaret Eddy for communal exegesis of the Bartimaeus story. They were used in various forms in different workshops, but they comprise a good overview of the process. Prior to this communal growing of the story, the group always learns the words of the story so that they can tell it with relative comfort.

1. Is the setting of Jericho important to Mark's telling of the story? Where is Jesus going, and for what purpose? What faith associations might Jericho have for first-century Christians?

2. Have the group look up Joshua, Chapters 2, 3, and 6; and II Kings, Chapter 2. Besides the location at or near Jericho, what theme do these stories have in common? Are there narrative threads, especially in II Kings 2, that connect with the Bartimaeus story?

3. What does the story tell us about Bartimaeus? How would you characterize him? Paint a verbal, visual picture of the scene.

4. What is the significance of Bartimaeus' cry in the first episode? (Background comment: This is the first time Mark has used the messianic title "Son of David" in his gospel. Jesus has only been referred to as "Son of Man," and by the demons, who are rebuked, as "Son of God.")

5. Why did many (crowd/disciples) rebuke Bartimaeus? What are the various possibilities? How has Mark used the "rebuke" theme throughout his gospel (leader may need to fill in briefly here)? What possible relationships do you see to Mark 8:31-33?

6. Have you ever experienced being rebuked? What is your most vivid memory? What was your response? What was Bartimaeus' response? What was Jesus' response in Mark 8:33?

7. What reversal of plot action do we find in the second episode in the calling? What are those who say "Take heart" doing? What are they projecting on Jesus?

8. In what ways have you been surprised by a change in people's attitudes towards you or your group? What dynamics caused the change?

9. What function does the mantle have in this story? What connections, similarities, and differences are there between Bartimaeus' mantle and the clothes and mantle in the Elijah-Elisha story (II Kings 2:8, 12-14)?

10. From a counseling or healing point of view, what is the significance of Jesus' question in the third episode (v. 51)?

11. Elijah asks this same question of Elisha (II Kings 2:9), and Jesus asks James and John, his disciples, this question in the preceding story (Mark 10:36). What contrasts or comparisons could Mark be trying to suggest to his audience?

12. Why is it important that we specify our need? If Jesus (or God or the Holy Spirit) asked you, "What do you want me to do for you?" what would you answer right now? What is your own most crucial

need? Take a moment right now and make a list of some of your needs. Then close your eyes and visualize yourself in the place of Bartimaeus in the story. See what answer comes from deep within now, when Jesus asks you the question.

13. What does Bartimaeus risk in asking for his sight? What are all the possible meanings of "sight" in this passage? Give as many synonyms as possible.

14. Just within this story, how has Bartimaeus shown his faith? Give concrete word images for the meaning of faith, just drawn from this text.

15. What instruction does Jesus give Bartimaeus? What does he actually do? Make up a little story of what might have happened next, on the way.

16. Early Christians were called "followers of the Way" (Acts 24:14). What would the implication of the last line be to them? How might they feel about Bartimaeus, in the light of their own political and social situation? What can be understood from this story about discipleship? (Eddy 1982, 133-35)

The value of this process for storytelling is that one finds a wide range of connections with the story from the experience of a whole community. Not only is the story enriched but also the common experience on which the community is based is broadened and deepened.

Telling the Story:
The Gospel as Storytelling in Worship

A principal occasion when the stories of the acts of God are told in the Church is public worship. The Scripture readings and the sermon are the two times in the service of the Word when the stories of the tradition are told in a variety of ways. And, in the Eucharistic liturgy, we retell the story of the institution of this holy meal.

The Scripture Lesson and Storytelling

The centrality of the narrative traditions of the Scriptures in the life of the community of Israel is reflected in the fact that the culmination of the Scriptural readings in both Judaism and Christianity is the reading of the sacred narratives. In Judaism, it is the Torah reading; in Christianity, the Gospel reading. The importance of the Gospel reading is dramatized in many parts of the Church by the congregation standing for the reading. And the liturgical actions of the taking of the Torah scroll from the Ark of the Covenant and the Gospel procession add further solemnity to the reading of the sacred stories in the synagogue and in some churches.

Just as reading stories to children in a library or at home is a form of storytelling, so also reading the sacred stories in worship is a form of storytelling. Unfortunately, these storytelling occasions have tended to become largely meaningless, especially within the Church, because of a lack of preparation and expectation on the part of both the readers and the listeners. Particularly in Protestant communities, the Scripture lesson has increasingly become a mere pretext for the sermon.

There are several reasons for this. One is the tradition of the monotone reading. For centuries in Christianity and still within the Orthodox Church and in Judaism, the Scriptures were always chanted. This chant was mellifluous and richly varied in its musical texture and melody. But, as the distance between the storytelling traditions and liturgical chant has increased, the chant has become more and more restricted in its musical range. This trend has culminated in the melody for cantillation becoming one note, a monotone. This mode of recital has come to be associated with a certain holiness and objectivity of presentation of the sacred stories. Unfortunately, it is often almost wholly devoid of meaning. People do not listen to the reading and it becomes a mere formal recital of words that we go through in order to get on to something meaningful.

In most of the Western Church, both Catholic and Protestant, the Scriptures are now read without chant. It has become common practice among both clerical and lay lectors that one prepares minimally or not at all for the reading of the Scriptures. And the result is predictable: no one, either reader or congregation, expects anything to happen during the reading of the Scriptures, and sure enough, nothing happens. The meaningfulness of the reading of the Scriptures in worship has largely died.

A source of renewal may be a recovery of the storytelling sources of public reading of the sacred narratives. Many pastors have found that memorizing and telling the Gospel narratives from memory has made the Scripture lessons more meaningful for the congregation. There is vitality and energy when the stories of the actions of God are told directly to the congregation without the presence of a manuscript or the formality of the lectern.

While I would not recommend this as a general practice, the reason is only that it takes a great deal of experience and skill to tell sacred stories well in public worship. But everyone who reads a biblical narrative in worship should memorize the story and learn its dynamics as a story as a preparation for reading the story in worship. The mode of recital will vary in its formality with the character of the congregation's liturgical life. But, regardless of the mode, the readings will only be meaningful to the listeners if they have first become meaningful to the person who is telling the story. Whether a manuscript and lectern are present is relatively insignificant in comparison to the centrality of preparation and emotional investment in the telling of the story. If a person has gone through the processes outlined in this book, the stories will be more meaningful and memorable when they are recited in public worship.

The Gospel as Storytelling and Preaching

The role of narratives in general and of the Gospel narratives in particular has been severely restricted in contemporary preaching. Biblical narratives have been reduced to a source of ideas or theological content for the sermon. And narratives in general have been reduced to serving as didactic illustrations for ideas. As a result, the Word of God has increasingly come to be associated with the theology that is abstracted out of the biblical tradition rather than with the experiencing of the biblical tradition itself. As a result, the Word of God has often come to be more closely associated with the sermon than with the Scriptures. In my experience of contemporary preaching, this association is ironic since the sermon is so often *in no apparent way* an expression of the Word of God. The

Scriptures, on the other, always have, at least potentially, a direct and perceivable relationship with God's Word.

This relationship between theological ideas and stories can be seen clearly in the typical structure of contemporary sermons:

Theme or central idea
Point 1 (development of some dimension of the idea)
   Illustration
Point 2 (further development of the idea)
   Illustration
Point 3
   Illustration
Closing summary

In this structure, the organizing principle of the sermon is the idea while the narratives serve as illustrations of the idea. The effect on narrative is that stories are only used as didactic tales that point to a moral or concretize an idea. This is a perfectly valid role for narrative. But when seen in the context of the rich range of narrative meanings, it is an impoverishment of its potential.

In no sense am I critical of this mode of preaching. It has been a means by which God's Word is authentically interpreted and made present for people now. And I am confident that it will continue to be.

But it is also possible to take the structure and promise of storytelling more seriously and to preach a sermon by retelling a biblical story. At the heart of this possibility is a reversal of the relationship between narrative and ideas. In a biblical narrative sermon, the structure of the narrative provides the structure and theological concepts make connections with the episodes of the story. In the Bartimaeus story, for example, an outline might be as follows:

Introduction: primary connection with the story
Bartimaeus's cry
   The experience of persons who are sick or oppressed
Jesus' response

134

The Christology of Jesus as God who hears our cries
The question and response
The importance of naming our need/prayer
The healing and Bartimaeus's following
Power of faith already present but unperceived; its
power in the history of the church and today.
Conclusion

Thus, in a story sermon, the structure of the story provides the structure of the sermon and theological ideas and contemporary experiences serve as ways of connecting the episodes of the story with contemporary thought. Rather than just outlining a theory, however, it might be helpful for me to give an example of such a story sermon. I preached the following sermon on Bartimaeus at the commencement of New York Theological Seminary, an interdenominational seminary that trains pastors for the rich variety of Christian communions in the New York metropolitan area.

The Cry of Faith

The story of Bartimaeus is a great story for a commencement because it is the story of the beginning of a whole new life. And I offer it to God and to each of you as a gift on this special day when we celebrate the commencement of new beginnings.

Let me tell you the story. Jesus had come down through the wilderness into Jericho, a tropical oasis near the Dead Sea, the deepest depression in the earth. And Jesus was leaving Jericho with a large crowd of followers. Now when Bartimaeus heard that it was Jesus of Nazareth, he started to cry out like a street corner preacher, "Son of David, Jesus, have mercy on me!" Bartimaeus didn't mess around trying to be sophisticated or cool. He mounted a one-man demonstration.

Well, the people who were standing around were embarrassed, and they told him to be quiet. "Shut up, Bartimaeus. He's a big deal rabbi. He's not going to pay any attention to you." It was a reflection on their personality as a town. They didn't want a beggar messing up their reputation. But

Bartimaeus kept on yelling all the louder, "Son of David, have mercy on me."

It was the cry of an oppressed man. He had been down, down so long that he almost couldn't hope any more. He was a victim, a victim of an accident of health. He had been able to see; the word at the end of the story means "to see again." But by some accident or illness he had been blinded and he couldn't see. And that took away his ability to work and his power. He had to become a beggar, humiliated, sitting in the dust. And he is one of so many people who are put down as the result of the accidents of history. It's humiliating to sit in the dust or in a gutter or in a bed as the result of an accident. It might have been the accident of an illness or a serious injury or physical handicap; or the accident of what sex you happened to be; or the accident of the color of your skin; or your economic status, how much money your parents had; or the kind of education that you were able to get. Accidents of history, but they are the accidents of history that are turned, by the powers of this world, into the means of oppression.

Bartimaeus may have been down but he was not out. He cried out a cry of faith. And what a man of faith he was, this blind beggar sitting in the dust. It is when you are down, I mean really down, that it's hardest to believe. It's when everything is going against you, when accidents of history continually beat you down. You try to stand up and you get knocked down again. It's far easier to sit there and be quiet, to let all those voices win that continually say, "Oh, shut up, be quiet, we don't want to hear it any more." But Bartimaeus didn't keep quiet. He cried out. And he didn't whine and say, "O Jesus, help; I'm so miserable." Nor did he demand and get tough with Jesus and say, "All right, Jesus, I demand that you get over here and heal me; I have been done unto and you have got to do something about it." No. He called out a prayer, a prayer that has become a part of the eucharistic liturgy: "Lamb of God, who takes away the sins of the world, have mercy on us." We should say his prayer as he said it; not as a cry of penitence, beating our breasts, but as a cry of faith for deliverance—"Son of David, Jesus, have mercy on me."

Let me give you theologians a test: was Bartimaeus a conservative or a liberal? Think with me for a moment.

You would have to admit that he is a conservative. He obviously believes in the possibility of faith healing. He also believes in the power of prayer. And this clinches it—he calls out that wonderful name, that great and powerful name of *Jesus*. A good paraphrase of his cry would be that cry that can be heard at many churches in this city: *"Help me, Jesus."* So Bartimaeus was a conservative.

But an equally good argument can be developed that he was a liberal. Bartimaeus was, after all, carrying on a non-violent direct action demonstration. He was engaged in a form of civil disobedience. He was actively advocating the needs of the blind. And, most important, notice that the first name that he called out is a political title, "son of David." Bartimaeus was involved in politics. Why, if the Romans had heard that, Jesus would have been in trouble. It was those kinds of cries that the chief priests cited as evidence in Jesus' trial before Pilate on that next Friday. Israel had hoped for generations for a "son of David" who would set them free from Gentile domination and reestablish the kingdom of David. Bartimaeus believed that Jesus was the Messiah. That's why he called him "son of David."

The cry of Bartimaeus can teach us something. Many of the divisions between conservatives and liberals in American Christianity must be transcended into a new synthesis. Christian social action without deeply rooted personal faith grounded in prayer, knowledge of the Scriptures, and regular worship will always be weak and short-lived. But a form of Christianity that seeks only to give individuals a personal experience of salvation is not Christianity. There are those who are saying that the churches had no business being involved in political and social issues in the sixties. But I say that nowhere in the Bible is there worship of a God who is only a personal God for individuals. Moses, the prophets, and Jesus were all involved in religious struggles that were profoundly political and affected the life of the nation of Israel. There is no dichotomy between religion and politics in the Bible. They are inextricably related. There are both individual and corporate aspects to the gospel. This seminary can forge a new unity between the various factions of American Christianity—conservatives and liberals, pentecostals and radicals. Look at your brothers and sisters in this community. They and those they represent are your primary allies in the struggle against the powers of evil in this age. The source of our unity can be heard in Bartimaeus's cry of faith.

Jesus stopped in the middle of the road and said, "Call him." And they said to Bartimaeus, "Take heart, get up, he's calling you." Well, he didn't stand up and stroll over to Jesus. He threw aside his cloak, jumped up, and came to Jesus. He didn't mess around; he got right in there. This was his chance.

Now how did Jesus hear him amidst all of the noise and distraction of his journey? Let me suggest that Jesus heard Bartimaeus's cry of faith because he had his ears finely tuned to hear the cries of the victims of the accidents of history. You might say that he kept his internal radio tuned to the PMBL network, that is, the station that broadcasts the cries of faith of the poor, the maimed, the blind, and the lame. But Jesus had to work to stay tuned to station PMBL because his disciples kept protecting him. The disciples often sought to keep people away from Jesus: mothers with children, followers of other rabbis, crazy types. Jesus had to work hard to keep from becoming insulated.

And graduates, you will have the same problem Jesus had. With a degree or a certificate goes status. And with status there are lots of good things. But there are also problems. People start to protect you. They say, "Well, she's awfully busy; she's got a degree." Or, "He's pretty smart and I don't know whether he will talk to me or not." Or, "I might be embarrassed; he probably won't have time." And so on. And many ministers do not stay tuned as Jesus did to those airwaves where they will hear the cries of faith from those who are hurting, from those who have been the victims of the accidents of history. Now I don't want to step on anybody's toes, but I note that many ministers listen mainly to station RHPR; that is, the rich, the healthy, the powerful, and the respectable. But Jesus stayed tuned to the PMBL network and those who would minister in his name have to keep their ears tuned to Jesus' favorite station. That is what liberation theology at its best is all about.

Jesus asked Bartimaeus, "What do you want me to do for you?" And Bartimaeus called him by his title because he respected him; "Rabboni, I want to see again." Bartimaeus didn't beat around the bush; he knew what he wanted.

And then Jesus did something very interesting. Rather, he didn't do something. He didn't lay hands on him or even touch him. He didn't put anything on his eyes or say any words of healing or exorcism. He didn't tell Bartimaeus *to do anything.* This is the only healing story like this. Can you see in your imagination how Jesus looked at him? And simply said, "Go, your faith has freed you." And immediately Bartimaeus could see again.

What had Jesus done? He had simply given permission to Bartimaeus's faith to become the power that set him free. Bartimaeus's cry of faith from the depths of his blindness liberated him from his affliction. Bartimaeus appeared to be weak, but by his faith in Jesus Christ he had the power of freedom in his own hands. And Jesus recognized the power in Bartimaeus's cry of faith and enabled that faith to go into action. And he could see again!

And what did he see? He saw that Jesus was the Messiah, that Jesus who was going up to Jerusalem to suffer and die was the Lord of heaven and earth, the chosen one of God.

Now the Church in America has been retreating from the period of social involvement in the sixties into private religion. And like Bartimaeus the Church does seem weak and powerless in comparison with the power of the government, the power of the commercial empires of the world, and especially the power of the combined armies of the world arming ever more powerfully for nuclear war. How do we feel by comparison? Weak. What is the power of the Church beside the powers of this world? It seems very small and insignificant.

But look at history through Bartimaeus's eyes. On Bartimaeus's commencement day, the power of Rome was overwhelming. A group of us have returned from a trip to the Holy Land and while we were there we saw the monuments of the Roman Empire. The most impressive was the wailing wall.

At the time of the Zealot war, the Romans were driven out of Israel for a year, but then they returned and systematically reoccupied the land. They besieged Jerusalem and destroyed the Temple.

Titus, the Roman general, left standing only one part of the outer wall of the Temple area. He left it there as a sign for all to see the power of Rome, of what Rome could destroy. And it was only the outer wall around the Temple. It rises up about one hundred feet and the rocks are massive. The Romans destroyed everything else. Their message: do not resist the power of Rome. And the armies of Israel could not.

But let me tell you a story. When Jesus died he left a group of followers—eleven disciples, perhaps two hundred followers at the most. Jesus left them with words and sacraments. When compared with the power of the Romans, the stories and sacraments of the Church seem relatively insignificant. But they are *not*. Jesus gave his disciples the essential means for setting free the power of faith.

And look at what has happened since Bartimaeus's day. We are a community of Christians in a continent that was not even known at the time of Jesus, and are part of a community of Christians that now extends to every part of the earth. Over the past two thousand years, the descendants of Bartimaeus have long since left Rome sitting in the dust. What did Rome amount to? Roughly three to four hundred years of power after the death of Jesus, and then Constantine gave in and became a Christian. Rome lost! Where is the power of Rome? Long dead, in the dust. Where is the power of the empires that have come and gone since then? Long dead. What remains of all the armies that have fought? Nothing, only the destruction that they have wrought. But the power of the gospel, the power of the story of Jesus, is now more powerful, touches more people's lives, than at any time in history.

Look at history through Bartimaeus's eyes. We have only begun to fight the battle of the Spirit. Look beyond our individual lives to the sweep of God's action in the life of the corporate community of the body of Christ and you, too, will see that the power of the kingdom of God in Jesus Christ will triumph over all the powers of oppression and evil.

Well, we are at the end of the story. Bartimaeus didn't go off and celebrate. He didn't say, "Whew, this begging has been hard work. I am going to take some time off and take it easy." He could see again, and he followed Jesus on the road to Jerusalem. This day is not an ending; it is a beginning. The degree is your marching orders. You have been enlisted in the band of the disciples of Jesus.

We have not been playing school. You have not been going through exercises or jumping through hoops in order to justify our giving you some credentials. We have been working together so that we can all be more powerful ministers of the faith of Bartimaeus. Therefore, remember Bartimaeus and the power of his cry of faith, and walk along with him and with all those disciples of Jesus who have gone before us and with those who will come after us, and we will all sing together on that great day of final victory the words of the old spiritual: "Free at last, free at last, thank God Almighty, we're free at last."

8

THE LAST SUPPER

(Mark 14:17-25)

The story of Jesus' passion, death, and resurrection is the climax of the gospel storytelling tradition. It is a story about the making and breaking of covenants between persons, between Jesus and God, and between God and humanity. The story of the last supper invites the listeners to experience Jesus' last meal intimately. In the context of his awareness and announcement of imminent betrayal by one of his disciples, Jesus makes covenant with them. The story sets all covenants, human and divine, in the context of God's covenant with us in Jesus' death and resurrection.

The Story

And when it was evening he came with the twelve.
And as they were reclining and eating, Jesus said, "Truly,
    I say to you, one of you will betray me, one who is
    eating with me."
They began to be sorrowful, and to say to him one after
    another, "Is it I?"

☆   ☆   ☆   ☆   ☆

He said to them, "It is one of the twelve, one who is
    dipping bread in the same dish with me.
For the Son of man goes as it is written of him, but woe to
    that man by whom the Son of man is betrayed!
It would have been better for that man if he had not been
    born."

☆ ☆ ☆ ☆ ☆

And as they were eating, he took bread, and blessed, and
    broke it, and gave it to them, and said, "Take.
This is my body."

☆ ☆ ☆ ☆ ☆

And he took a cup, and when he had given thanks he gave
    it to them, and they all drank of it.
And he said to them, "This is my blood of the covenant,
    which is poured out for many.
Truly, I say to you, I shall not drink again of the fruit of
    the vine until that day when I drink it new in the
    kingdom of God."

Learning the Story

Verbal Threads

"**The twelve.**" Both episodes of the betrayal prophecy have
this phrase: "He came with the twelve"/"one of the twelve"
(vss. 17, 20). It is Jesus' name for those who were his disciples
and closest friends.

"**As they were reclining and eating.**" The two stories of the
supper—the betrayal and the interpretation of the bread and
wine—are connected by this introductory phrase (vss. 18, 22).
Jesus' prophecy of the betrayal is introduced by the phrase
literally translated "as they were reclining and eating," while
the setting for the supper has the abbreviated form of the verbal
thread, "as they were . . . eating."

"**One of.**" A typical verbal thread is formed by the
introduction of this phrase, "one of you" (vs. 18), which is
combined with the opening thread "the twelve" (vs. 17) to form

the phrase which names the scandal that Jesus is betrayed by one *so* intimate, by "one of the twelve" (vs. 20).

"That man." The only other verbal connection in the prophecy of the betrayal is "that man," which describes the betrayer (vs. 21 *a, b*). The phrase expresses the distance and alienation from Jesus that Judas' betrayal has caused.

"Took . . . he gave it to them . . . and said . . . 'This is my.' " This extensive verbal thread is the verbal tie between the two episodes of the supper story (vss. 22-23). It is also the climactic conclusion of the motif of Jesus' blessing at sacramental meals that was established in the two earlier stories of the feedings in the wilderness (Mark 6:41; 8:6).

This is one of the simplest stories in the gospel tradition in its form and structure. There are no real changes in the scene or developments of the plot. The two parts of the supper story deal with the betrayal of the covenant between Jesus and his disciples and the establishment of covenant between them in his gift of the bread and the wine. Each part has two episodes that develop the theme first of the betrayal and then of the bread and wine.

Listening to the Story

Nowhere else in the gospel narrative does a prophecy follow the first steps of its fulfillment. Just prior to the story of the preparations for Passover, Mark has reported Judas' trip to the chief priests in order to betray Jesus (14:10-11). The verbal threads—"betray" ("hand over") (vss. 10-11, 18, 21) and especially "one of the twelve" (vss. 10, 20)—make the connection between this betrayer and Judas unmistakable for the listener. The context of Jesus' prophecy is the time of greatest intimacy in the entire religious year, the Passover meal.

Mark graphically delineates this context by drawing out a series of highly emotional associations with earlier memories from the story. "When it was evening" is associated in the earlier narrative with times of fellowship and retreat for Jesus and the disciples (the boat trip, 4:35; the trip out to Bethany, 11:11).

"The twelve" were Jesus' disciples, the students whom he had taught in his traveling seminary. All of the memories of the events they had shared are caught up in this term. The particular character of their relationship is concretized in the story of the Passover preparations that precedes the betrayal prophecy (14:12-16). The agreement between disciples and rabbis was that the rabbi would teach them in exchange for help in the provision of his basic needs. The disciples were, therefore, acting appropriately when they asked Jesus where they should prepare the Passover meal for him. All of the warmth and commitment of their relationship is present in the disciples' preparation of the Passover meal for their rabbi. The setting creates the anticipation of an evening of intimate fellowship and festive celebration in eating the Passover meal together.

This setting is reinforced by the description of the meal itself: "as they were reclining and eating" (vs. 18). Reclining to eat was normal in Jesus' day. But Mark only uses the word *anakeimai* ("to recline") one other time, in his description of Herod's guests at the birthday party when Herod had John beheaded (6:26). In both instances, the image of reclining draws a picture of a festive banquet, at which violence and betrayal become the main event. Thus, Mark establishes an atmosphere of convivial good cheer as the context for Jesus' prophecy of betrayal by one of the twelve.

Jesus announces the prophecy twice. In both statements, the betrayer is named in two ways: first, in terms of the covenant of rabbi and disciple, and, second, in terms of the covenant of table fellowship: "one of you"/"one of the twelve," "one who is eating with me"/"one who is dipping bread in the same dish with me." The description of these covenants is a crescendo of scandal. The degree of offense is hard for contemporary storytellers to feel. First, it was virtually unthinkable for a disciple to betray the covenant with his rabbi. It is like a soldier shooting his commanding officer in the back during battle.

But the greatest emphasis is given to Judas' betrayal of the covenant of table fellowship. This covenant was supremely sacred in the ancient Near East. A person would do almost anything to avoid violating that covenant. The centrality of that covenant is reflected in a number of stories in Genesis and Judges. The connection between making covenants and sharing table fellowship is evident in the stories of Isaac's covenant with Abimelech (Gen. 26:28-30) and Jacob's covenant with Laban (Gen. 31:43-54). The most graphic stories of the violation of the covenant are the two stories of assault on a visiting guest: (1) the attack by the men of Sodom on the angels who were visiting the city and had been welcomed into Lot's house (Gen. 19:1-11), and (2) the rape and murder by men from the tribe of Benjamin of an Israelite woman, a concubine who with her husband was a guest in the town of Gibeah (Judg. 19). In both instances, the punishment for their outrageous crimes was extreme. Sodom was destroyed by fire and brimstone and all of Israel attacked the tribe of Benjamin and killed thousands of Benjaminite men (Judg. 20). The tribe of Benjamin never fully recovered from this disaster.

In both instances, the men who had welcomed the guests appealed to the laws of hospitality and table fellowship (Gen. 19:8; Judg. 19:23). In the world of biblical narrative, the horror and revulsion that the stories of these crimes elicit is appropriately associated with violations of the covenant of hospitality and table fellowship. The memory of these most despicable crimes in the history of Israel is an appropriate connection with Judas' betrayal.

Jesus' response is to recognize the horrible judgment that the betrayer's crime would bring upon him, a judgment not unlike that which fell on Sodom and the Benjaminites. The pronouncement of "woe" is an ancient prophetic tradition of sharing beforehand the fate of one who is going to endure great suffering (e.g., I Kings 13:20-32). The spirit of Jesus' words is not then to condemn Judas but is rather to recognize and to share his impending suffering. Jesus contrasts his own coming death in fulfillment of the will of God with Judas' coming disaster in violation of God's will.

The audience can judge, therefore, that Judas' action was not divinely determined and that he stands under divine judgment. The story appeals for a high degree of sympathy with Jesus in his grief. And because of the story's structure, the listeners can confirm that Jesus' prophecy is true.

147

This prophecy of betrayal is the immediate context for Jesus' reinterpretation of the bread and wine of the Passover meal as his body and blood. Jesus' response to this violation of covenant is to make a new covenant with his disciples including, by implication, even the betrayer. The expected response to the violation of covenant is reflected in the Judges story: outrage and punishment. Jesus' response is radically different.

The warmth and fellowship of the meal is reestablished in the introduction of the setting, "as they were . . . eating." The distribution of the bread has an extensive verbal connection with the earlier feeding stories in Mark:

> The feeding of the five thousand—*"And taking* the five *loaves* and the two fish he looked up to heaven, *and blessed, and broke* the loaves, *and gave* them to the disciples to set before the people" (6:41).
> The feeding of the four thousand—*"And he took* the seven *loaves,* and having given thanks *he broke them and gave them* to his disciples to set before the people" (8:6).
> The Last Supper—*"He took bread, and blessed, and broke it, and gave* it to them" (14:22).

In each of these earlier feedings stories, Mark has developed the motif of disciples' misunderstanding of the loaves (e.g., see 6:52 and especially 8:17-21). The culmination of this motif in the plot is Jesus' speech as a highly frustrated teacher whose students don't understand:

And being aware of it, Jesus said to them, "Why do you discuss the fact that you have no bread? Do you not yet perceive or understand? Are your hearts hardened? Having eyes do you not see, and having ears do you not hear? And do you not remember? When I broke the five loaves for the five thousand, how many baskets full of broken pieces did you take up?" They said to him, "Twelve." "And the seven for the four thousand, how many baskets full of broken pieces did you take up?" And they said to him, "Seven." And he said to them, "Do you not yet understand?" (Mark 8:17-21)

It is important for prospective storytellers to recognize the function of this speech in Mark's narrative. Not only do the disciples not understand, the information is not given in the story that would enable the listeners to understand either. The puzzle of the meaning of the loaves remains throughout the narrative until this moment in the story. It is a classic mystery story technique. Jesus' words—"Take; this is my body"—are the solution to the mystery of the loaves. The bread that was miraculously multiplied was and is Jesus' body. Jesus had given himself to the crowds and to the disciples.

The second episode of the supper is Jesus' reinterpretation of the Passover wine and his vow of abstinence from wine. The only major verbal link with earlier motifs in Mark's Gospel is the introductory formula. Jesus' reinterpretation of the meaning of the Passover wine has one major link to the tradition of Israel. In the story of the covenant between Yahweh and Israel at Sinai, the covenant is sealed by the sprinkling of the blood of the oxen on the people: "And Moses took the blood and threw it upon the people and said, 'Behold the blood of the covenant which the Lord has made with you in accordance with all these words' " (Exod. 24:8). Thus, Jesus links the wine with his blood and with the blood of the Mosaic covenant. By analogy, therefore, Jesus is a human sacrifice whose death seals the new covenant, just as the sacrifice of oxen sealed the covenant in the Exodus story.

The climax of the story is Jesus' vow of abstinence from wine until the coming of the kingdom. The background of such vows in Israel can be seen in the story of Uriah, the husband of Bathsheba. When Bathsheba became pregnant after David took her, Uriah was called back from the battlefields for a leave during which he would presumably sleep with her and cover David's tracks. But Uriah slept at the door of the king's house. When David asked him about this, Uriah said:

The ark and Israel and Judah dwell in booths; and my lord Joab and the servants of my lord are camping in the open field; shall I then go to my house, to eat and to drink, and to lie with my wife? As you live, and as your soul lives, I will not do this thing. (II Sam. 11:11)

Uriah's refusal is an expression of his faithfulness to the vow of abstinence taken by soldiers consecrated for war (see also I Sam. 21:4-5). Thus, at the end of the meal, Jesus takes a vow of abstinence as a consecration of himself for his struggle. The vow of abstinence from wine is a Nazirite vow which has a long and rich tradition in Israel (Num. 6:1-4; Judg. 13:4-5; I Sam. 1:11; Amos 2:11-12).

The dynamics of this story are to be found in the depths of the most solemn covenant traditions of Israel. This last supper is a time of solemn vows. This new covenant is made in the context of Jesus' recognition of the betrayal of the covenant by one of his disciples. Knowing that one of the twelve is betraying him, Jesus makes covenant with them. Ordinarily, a betrayer is to be exposed and expelled. But Jesus protects his betrayer's identity and makes covenant with him as well as the others. Jesus gives himself even for the trusted one who has made himself Jesus' enemy. The impact of this story lies in the unspoken depths of its passion. To a unique degree, its meaning is known in the slow intensity of the words and the silences that plumb the depths of God's covenant.

Connections

The appropriate telling of this story is simple and direct. Our connection to the dynamics of the story is our experiences of making and breaking covenants. But the words of Jesus are difficult. How can we appropriately render Jesus' words in this story? It is the intimidating nature of this question that has led to monotone recitals in which the words of Jesus sound like a computer or a robot. The chant of the ancient tradition is one solution. But chanting is a strange and alien modality for the dominant cultures of the Western world. If, therefore, Jesus' words are to be experienced as those of a human being, they must in some sense express human emotions.

The connection with the prophecy of the betrayal is the experience of being let down or hurt by someone whom you have loved and trusted. Therefore, your deepest experiences of betrayal are your link with this story. Remembering and retelling those stories can provide a context for telling Jesus' story and for rethinking your own experience. If you have a partner, I would suggest that you do that. When has someone whom you loved and trusted broken covenant with you? Tell that story and then tell the story of Jesus' last supper. Also when have you broken a covenant that you made with someone who loved and trusted you? Listening to the story in this context may shed new light on both sides of your covenantal relationships.

There are many other potential connections with the last supper story: good-byes, last holidays together, festive mealtimes. But the primary connection is with the times of making covenant: marriages, baptisms, ordinations, installations, inaugurations, and the swearing of oaths in court. What are your primary memories of making covenant? Those occasions at their deepest level are the most direct link to the dynamics of the supper narrative.

Few words are spoken in making covenants. At these times, words *do* something rather than just convey a meaning. Paying attention to what these covenant words do links us with what matters in Jesus' story and in our own. Experiencing our covenants in the context of God's covenant with us in Christ puts our covenants in good light.

Telling the Story

The sharing of this story is an opportunity to invite persons into a new relationship: with God, with others, and with themselves. In the Christian community, the primary occasion when we tell this story is the Eucharist or Holy Communion. Unfortunately, our celebrations of the sacrament are often so distant in their remembrance of the story and in their connection with our covenants that they become meaningless. The Eucharist as a time of covenant renewal is often remote or absent. And the story is often buried in the liturgical formulae.

Is there an approach to Eucharist that grows out of the storytelling tradition? I offer here a few suggestions. The story of the supper in the Gospels is always associated with the breaking of covenant. The story invites us then to bring those experiences of the breaking of covenant to the celebration of covenant making. The covenants have two dimensions: first, covenants between God and us, and, second, our covenants with other persons.

The impact of Jesus' gift of himself is tied to the realization that I might be the betrayer. The story thus invites us to bring to the sacrament our own examined memories of those times and manners in which we have broken covenant with God. Preparation for receiving communion has always included some rite of penance. In the liturgy of the Episcopal/Methodist tradition, this was expressed in the prayer of humble access. In current ecumenical liturgies, communion is immediately preceded by the recital of the centurion's word: "Lord, I am not worthy to receive you, but only say the word and I shall be healed." But these words are most meaningful if they express some awareness of the current condition of my covenant with God.

In what ways have you broken covenant with God? That may mean ceasing to believe or trust in God's power or faithfulness. It might be related to dissociating from God and establishing greater distance. Or it may mean being angry with God for asking you to be faithful through suffering and death.

I find that the feeling also is present sometimes that God has broken covenant with me. For example, when sudden suffering or an unexpected death occurs, it feels as if God is not keeping God's promises. Examining this apparent breach of covenant makes it clear that the covenant God has broken was one I developed. The contract was that I would do certain "religious" things with the assumption that God would do certain things for me, such as protecting me and those I love from sudden suffering or unexpected death. If I am afflicted or grieved, the feeling is that God has forsaken me and is not being faithful to the covenant between us. Granted, this may not be a covenant God either proposed or entered into, at least as I have defined it. Nevertheless, those feelings are present and are connected in some way with this story. Such aspects of our covenant with

God can be shared with God or with another person prior to the covenant meal.

The covenant meal also recalls to us our broken covenants with those who have loved and trusted us. In what ways have you broken covenant with those who have loved and trusted you? In some way, either in prayer or in dialogue with a minister or priest or a spiritual companion, it is appropriate to acknowledge our own fracturing of covenants. The sharing of the peace prior to the receiving of the sacred meal is an opportunity for reconciliation of our covenants that have either been fractured or just stressed. But, regardless of the ways, the gift of the story of the last supper is most fully received in the context of these relationships.

Therefore, the sacrament and the telling of these holy tales have the same function. They are the means by which God is present with us. The words of the story and the actions of the sacrament mutually reinforce and strengthen each other. The gifts of God are uniquely present in these simple means of grace.

Storytelling and Religious Education

While Jesus' last supper is the most frequently remembered narrative in the Christian community, few Christians actually learn to tell the actual story. In fact, children and adults are seldom taught to tell any of the biblical stories. There are values inherent in the biblical storytelling tradition that can strengthen the Church's educational work.

The basic model of a storytelling process in education is simple. Children hear the stories from adults, first their parents and grandparents and then other significant adults in the family or community. They learn the stories from repetition and study. As they grow up, the children are encouraged and rewarded for developing their own abilities to tell the stories. When they become adults, they tell the stories to their children as well as to others in the community.

Biblical storytelling is, therefore, a foundational process in religious education at all levels. The reason is that biblical storytelling is a primary language of faith. In the process of mastering this language, both the individual and the community are formed. Learning to tell biblical stories is good for the growing of healthy persons and communities.

Rather than outlining a programmatic model, I want to describe some of the values of approaching the gospel as storytelling in education. A pedagogy based on the values of storytelling can give life to Christian education at all levels.

The Intimacy of the Spoken Word

When the stories are told by adults who love them, the sound of the stories creates resonance, "vibes," between adults and children. Rather than the distant analysis of printed texts, storytelling, when done well, is alive and vibrant. The love of God, for example, is then understood by the nuances of meaning that are communicated through the voice.

The Nurture of Memory

The elimination of memorization in religious education or the restriction of memorization to individual verses of Scripture or answers to catechetical questions impoverishes the tradition. We recognize how traumatic the loss of memory is for a person with Alzheimer's disease. But, as a religious community, we have so minimized the nurture of our communal memory that the Church suffers from a kind of amnesia, with all its symptoms: disorientation, insecurity, immobilization and inability to act, and a lack of confidence.

The deepest effect of minimizing memorization of the tradition is on internalization. When the stories of the Gospels are no longer known "by heart," the knowledge of the events of Jesus' life, death, and resurrection is superficial and relatively unimportant. The stories are associated with concepts but are dissociated from feelings and the resonances of primary experience. They are inadequately interiorized. Poets, dramatists, and musicians who live in the world of sound know that only those traditions that have been deeply internalized can be understood and performed well.

154

The effect of this elimination can be seen in the graduates of the Church's educational system. The graduates of our programs are often familiar with a wide range of knowledge, but know little in depth. A recovery of storytelling as a means for the internalization of the principal Christian traditions would help to minimize this problem. The elimination of aural memory from the pedagogical process in most mainline Protestant churches may help to explain the decline of the educational programs of those churches. Catholics, who have only in recent years begun to emphasize biblical study in religious education for both children and adults, would do well to learn from the Protestant experience.

Community Formation

Storytelling is a potential source of renewal for the two basic educational communities of the Church: the family and the congregation. In both communities, the loss of a deeply internalized and broadly based communal memory grounded in the stories of the actions of God has been a source of weakness.

The family has been the primary center of education throughout the history of Israel and the Church. In Israel and the early Church, parents were expected to tell the stories to their children. In Protestantism, families gathered for the weekly or daily reading of the Scriptures. For Catholics, the family rosary with its fifteen mysteries or meditations on events in Christ's life passed on the memory of those events. The role of parents in religious education has always been closely connected with some form of biblical recital or prayer. This has involved reading or telling the narratives of the Scriptures or leading the family in prayer and meditation on the events of Jesus' life. But, with the decline of oral recitation, the role of the family and parents in the educational process has declined.

An important step in the revitalization of religious education may be, therefore, to enable parents to learn and tell the stories to their children. The most natural time for this training is prior to the birth and baptism of their children. I would suggest that a constituent part of the preparation for parents who want to have their children baptized might be a period of training and education in storytelling.

One of the values of such training is to prepare women and men for the crises of parenting. I remember one night when my eight-year-old was unable to settle down because of a recurring nightmare about a ghost. It was near Halloween and ghosts were in the air. In response to his cries—"Dad, I can't go to sleep! I'm scared!"—I first tried to lighten the atmosphere: "Come on. You know that ghosts don't exist. They are only imaginary. Just say 'Hi' or imagine that it is like Casper." After a little while, he said, "I tried that. I'm still scared." When the lightening-the-atmosphere approach didn't work, I tried threats: "If you don't settle down in three minutes . . . " You can imagine how effective that was.

I then went upstairs and told him the story of Jesus walking on the water, how in the middle of the night the disciples saw him walking on the water and cried out, "It's a ghost." And how Jesus said, "Be not afraid. I am." (This was during the era of "Happy Days" and the Fonz; so I did a sort of Fonzie interpretation of Jesus' words, with my thumbs up: "Hey, don't be afraid. I am in charge." That cracked him up.) I told him how Jesus got into the boat and that, suddenly, there was a great calm. And how Jesus had said, "O men of little faith, why were you afraid? Have you no faith?" (Apparently my son could accept virtually the same words I had said earlier when they came from Jesus in the story.) After I finished the story, he sighed a big sigh, as if a big load had been taken off his shoulders, and said, "Thanks, Dad." And after a hug, he rolled over and went fast asleep.

In addition to telling the stories, parents also need to enable their children to learn to tell the stories themselves. This will in part be the natural result of frequent tellings. One of my earliest memories is learning to recite " 'Twas the Night before Christmas" when I was four years old. I required my mother to read it to me over and over again. And through sheer repetition, I was soon able at the age of three or four to astound my Aunt Mary by reciting the whole thing. I used to tell this story with pride. I now know that many Hasidic children have learned the entire books of Genesis and Exodus in Hebrew by the time they are four. Nevertheless, there is no doubt that this early experience has been a source of my interest in storytelling.

What my mother and aunt did was in direct continuity with the basic principles of Suzuki education. This pedagogical genius has taught young children from all over the world to play the violin with a degree of facility that is truly incredible. The principle is simple. Children are rewarded by praise at every stage of learning to play the violin. And the parents are required to be involved with the entire process of their child's learning. But their most important job is to provide positive reinforcement.

Suzuki developed the basic principles of his method by observing how Japanese children accomplish a remarkable learning task by the age of four: they have all learned to speak Japanese. He observed that the way parents teach their children to speak Japanese is by constant positive reinforcement. A child says "Mama" (or its Japanese equivalent), and the mother responds happily with big smiles, hugs, and as soon as father comes home, a command performance. And if the child says it again, there will be more smiles, hugs, and celebrations from the father.

A Suzuki recital is a wonder and a joy to behold. One child, who has just begun the program, steps up and bows—that's all, just a bow. And everyone applauds. Another steps up, puts the violin under her chin in the correct position and places the bow on the strings; then she bows. And everyone applauds. Each child performs at the level he or she has mastered, from the most simple to the most complex. And everyone applauds! This basic process is continued at all stages. Corrections of notes and technique are made by the teachers along the way. But corrections are always made in the context of affirmation and positive reinforcement.

The same process works with all ages of persons who are learning to tell biblical stories. Begin with small efforts, such as having them tell a story from personal experience. Next, teach them a short biblical story and have them tell it to another person, perhaps with puppets or clay or a picture. Have them

157

learn another story, somewhat longer, and tell it to a group of four. And after some time, the students will be able to tell long stories with real skill and confidence, either in congregational worship or in storytelling occasions of various kinds, such as visits to hospitalized church members.

Every time a story is told becomes a sacramental occasion. It is a sign of the presence of God in the midst of the community. But those signs are of particular delight and joy when the storytellers are persons who are not normally expected to tell stories. Storytelling is the language of the people. Each person's gift to the storytelling tradition is distinctive and precious. And the celebration of those gifts in the life of the family and the community is a joyful thing. It is a source of covenant renewal.

9

CRUCIFIXION

(Mark 15:21-41)

The story of Jesus' crucifixion is a complex and multifaceted martyr story. The story describes a violent, unjust execution with emotional restraint. There are no maudlin details, such as can be heard regularly in retellings of this story. Nevertheless, the injustice and agony of Jesus' death are described in a manner that is unforgettable. The story sets our experiences of human captivity to the powers of sin and death in the context of this death.

The Story

And they compelled a passer-by, Simon of Cyrene, who
    was coming in from the country, the father of
    Alexander and Rufus, to carry his cross.
And they brought him to the place called Golgotha
    (which means the place of a skull).

☆ ☆ ☆ ☆ ☆

And they offered him wine mingled with myrrh.
But he did not take it.

☆ ☆ ☆ ☆ ☆

159

And they crucified him, and divided his garments among
them, casting lots for them, to decide what each
should take.
And it was the third hour, when they crucified him.

☆ ☆ ☆ ☆ ☆

And the inscription of the charge against him read, "The
King of the Jews."
And with him they crucified two robbers, one on his right
and one on his left.

☆ ☆ ☆ ☆ ☆

And those who passed by derided him, wagging their
heads, and saying, "Aha! You who would destroy
the temple and build it in three days.
Save yourself, and come down from the cross!"

☆ ☆ ☆ ☆ ☆

So also the chief priests mocked him to one another with
the scribes, saying, "He saved others; he cannot save
himself.
Let the Christ, the King of Israel, come down now from
the cross, that we may see and believe."
Those who were crucified with him also reviled him.

☆ ☆ ☆ ☆ ☆

And when the sixth hour had come, there was darkness
over the whole land until the ninth hour.
And at the ninth hour Jesus cried with a loud voice, "Eloi,
Eloi, lama sabachthani?"
Which means, "My God, my God, why have you forsaken
me?"

☆ ☆ ☆ ☆ ☆

And some of the bystanders hearing it said, "Look, he is
calling Elijah."
And one ran and, filling a sponge full of vinegar, put it on
a reed and gave it to him to drink, saying, "Wait, let
us see whether Elijah will come to take him down."

But Jesus uttered a loud cry, and breathed his last.

☆　☆　☆　☆　☆

And the curtain of the temple was torn in two, from top to
bottom.

And when the centurion, who stood facing him, saw that
he thus breathed his last, he said, "Truly, this man
was the Son of God!"

There were also women looking on from afar, among
whom were Mary Magdalene, and Mary the mother
of James the younger and of Joses, and Salome, who,
when he was in Galilee, followed him, and minis-
tered to him, and also many other women who came
up with him to Jerusalem.

Learning the Story

Verbal Threads

"Crucified." The crucifixion section of the story is linked by
the verb "to crucify." Literally translated, the crucifixion
verbal threads alternate between present and past tenses. "And
they crucify him" (vs. 24); "Now it was the third hour and they
crucified him" (vs. 25); "And with him they crucify" (vs. 27).
This last verbal thread is picked up as the climax of the mocking
episode: "those crucified with him" (vs. 32).

"Save yourself, and come down from the cross." The two
parts of this mocking statement made by those who passed by
are picked up and developed in the statement of the chief
priests and scribes: "He saved others; he cannot save himself.
Let the Christ . . . come down now from the cross" (vss.
31-32*a*). This connection is the verbal component for the
crescendo of mockery in this episode.

"A loud voice"/"cry." The episodes of the death story begin
and end with the verbal thread of Jesus' cry. The cry of
dereliction is introduced by the phrase literally rendered "Jesus
cried out with a loud cry" (vs. 34). And the moment of death

uses these same words: "Jesus, giving a loud cry" (vs. 37).

"Look, he is calling Elijah." The motif of the mockery and misunderstanding of Jesus' cry by those at the foot of the cross is introduced by this phrase. The verbal thread concludes with the statement of the one who gave him the sour wine, "Let us see whether Elijah will come" (vss. 35-36).

Listening to the Story

The preparation for the execution has two themes: the journey to Golgotha and the offer of the wine. The description of Simon of Cyrene (15:21) is highly personal. The naming of his sons, ("the father of Alexander and Rufus") implies that the narrator knows his family and thereby makes him a sympathetic character. The offer of the wine receives the greatest emphasis because of the shortness of the sentences. This offer is verbally connected with the last supper. Thus, a more literal translation of this verbal thread from the Greek is as follows:

And . . . *taking* bread . . . he *gave* it to them and said, *"Take it."* And *taking* a cup . . . he *gave* it to them. (14:22-23)

And they *gave* him wine mingled with myrrh; but he did not *take* it. (15:23)

This connection contrasts sharing bread and wine at the Passover meal with the offer of wine at the crucifixion. The linkage with the last supper also answers the question implicit in Jesus' refusal of the wine: why didn't he take it? The conclusion to the supper was Jesus' vow of abstinence from wine. His refusal is, therefore, tied to his vow. Jesus keeps his vow of abstinence at the cost of even greater pain (15:23).

The description of the crucifixion focuses first on Jesus' garments. It is linked to the end of the mocking by the soldiers. The Greek text here can be translated "after they had finished mocking him, they put his own garments *back* on him" (Mark 15:20). In the crucifixion, they divided "his garments." The storyteller thereby implies that, once again, they stripped him naked. There was no greater shame in Israel.

This description of the dividing of his garments is in turn a quotation of Psalm 22:19 (Ps. 21 in the Greek Septuagint). The following translation makes clear this connection in the Greek texts:

They divided my garments among themselves and upon my garment they cast lots. (Ps. 22:19)

They divided his garments casting lots on them to see who would take what. (Mark 15:24)

Psalm 22 is a lament. This reference indicates the emotional tone in which the story was told.

The reports of the time of the crucifixion and the inscription of the charge (vss. 25-26) are narrative comments. The storyteller interrupts the story to give the listeners these pieces of background information. Mark reports the crucifixion twice, each time in a different tense. As was noted above, in the Greek the first description is in the present tense—"and they crucify him"—while the second is in the aorist or past tense—"Now it was the third hour and they crucified him." The crucifixion is thus reported from two perspectives. The first time the narrator is an eyewitness who describes the crucifixion as it takes place, now. We are there. In the second report, the storyteller stops the story and speaks directly to his listeners in the present moment of the telling of the story. This is a retrospective account from the perspective of a person years later looking back on the event.

While we cannot hear how Mark said these words, the text suggests that they were spoken with some combination of horror, grief, irony, and disbelief. Repetitions are only made in biblical narrative in order to build a climax and to express a full range of emotions. Thus, the first description expresses the horror of watching the crucifixion happen, now. The second conveys the narrator's own disbelief and grief at what is happening. The second is shorter and, therefore, more deliberate and emotionally expressive. And, as with all narrative comments, the storyteller takes time to look directly at his listeners and to share with them.

The descriptions of the charge against Jesus and of his crucifixion with "robbers" are bitterly ironic (15:26). The title "King of the Jews" was only used by the chief priests in the trial before Pilate and by the Roman soldiers during the mocking inside the praetorium. To the high priest's question, "Are you the Christ, the Son of the Blessed?" Jesus responded positively, "I am" (14:61-62). By contrast, his response to Pilate's question, "Are you the King of the Jews?" was an equivocation: "You say it" (15:2). In Mark's story, Jesus never claims to be king. The implication is that this political charge was trumped up in order to get him condemned. And the fact that it is used by the Roman soldiers increases the irony. All of this indicates the tone in which the description of the charge was reported by the ancient narrator. The charge was unjust. Jesus was innocent. The tone was outrage, bitter irony.

The climax of the irony is that he was crucified with two "robbers," on his right and his left. In the original Greek, the storyteller goes back to the present tense of the eyewitness after his comments to the listeners: "And with him, they crucify . . . " (15:27). The Greek word here, usually translated "robbers" *(lastas),* was often used to describe "brigands" or "political bandits," and particularly the Jewish revolutionaries who led the revolt against the Romans in A.D. 66–70. In Mark's context, during or shortly after the war, the connection of this term with the revolutionaries would have been current. Furthermore, the phrase "on the right and the left" has been used earlier in the story by James and John when they requested positions of power (10:37, 40). The irony is that those who are crucified on Jesus' right and left are not his friends reigning with him but revolutionaries dying with him. In Jesus' case, to be executed in association with a revolution that he implicitly opposed was supremely ironic.

The culmination of this crescendo of irony is the mocking of Jesus on the cross (15:29-32). Prior to this, Jesus has been mocked by the enemies of Israel, the Romans. But now he is mocked by the people, the most respected leaders of the nation, and even by those who are crucified with him. The irony is experienced most fully against the background of the Jewish martyr stories, such as the story in II Maccabees of the seven boys. The boys supported each other. As they died, they encouraged one another.

The "wagging" of the head indicates the gesture of the storyteller as he describes those who passed by the cross. It is a further allusion to Psalm 22: "All who see me mock at me,/they make mouths at me, they wag their heads (vs. 7). In the tradition of Israel, wagging the head is a sign of scorn and derision (Sir. 12:18; 13:7; Job 16:4).

Once again, as with the inscription, the mockers refer to a charge against Jesus that has been shown to be false. This false charge was brought by the false witnesses at Jesus' trial before the Sanhedrin:

And some stood up and bore false witness against him, saying, "We heard him say, 'I will destroy this temple that is made with hands, and in three days I will build another, not made with hands.' " (14:57-58)

The words of the mockers at the cross are "You who would destroy the temple and build it in three days" (15:2, 9). The implication is that they are condemning him for the charge brought against him at the trial, a charge that the storyteller has already made clear is a false charge.

The chief priests and scribes pick up and elaborate the themes of the mockers passing by. They refer back to the other titles for which Jesus was condemned in the two trials: "the Christ" (14:61) and "the King of the Jews" (15:2, 9). The second title is slightly modified to "the King of Israel" (vs. 33). From the narrator's point of view, the chief priests and scribes, the most respected leaders of Israel, here commit what can only be called blasphemy. They slander and mock the Lord's Messiah.

The final culmination of this litany of mockery is that Jesus is reviled by the men who are crucified with him. From the leaders to the bandits, representatives of the entire nation mock Jesus. In fact, the mockery by the people of Israel is both more violent and receives more emphasis in the narrative than the mockery and humiliation of Jesus by the Gentile Roman soldiers.

The problem in telling this story is that contemporary Christian storytellers tend to tell or read this story with an attitude of hostility and judgment toward Jews. The effect of the telling of the stories is often to place the blame for Jesus' death on them, as if they were the enemy.

In order to hear this story in its original context, it needs to be heard in relation to the stories of other prophet martyrs in the tradition of Israel. The story of the martyrdom of Isaiah is the most illuminating. This story was probably written during the Maccabean period approximately two hundred years before Mark. I would suggest that you read it aloud:

And while Isaiah was being sawed in half, his accuser, Belkira, stood by, and all the false prophets stood by, laughing and (maliciously) joyful because of Isaiah. And Belkira through Mekembekus, stood before Isaiah, laughing and deriding. And Belkira said to Isaiah, "Say, 'I have lied in everything I have spoken; the ways of Manasseh are good and right, and also the ways Belkira and those who are with him are good.' " And he said this to him when he began to be sawed in half.

And Isaiah was in a vision of the Lord, but his eyes were open, and he saw them. And Belkira spoke thus to Isaiah, "Say what I say to you, and I will turn their heart and make Manasseh, and the princes of Judah, and the people, and all Jerusalem worship you." And Isaiah answered and said, "If it is within my power to say, 'Condemned and cursed be you, and all your hosts and all your house!' For there is nothing further that you can take except the skin of my body."

And they seized Isaiah the son of Amoz and sawed him in half with a wood saw. And Manasseh, and Belkira, and the false prophets, and the princes, and the people, and all stood by looking on. And to the prophets who were with him he said before he was sawed in half, "Go to the district of Tyre and Sidon, because for me alone the Lord has mixed the cup." And while Isaiah was being sawed in half, he did not cry out, or weep, but his mouth spoke with the Holy Spirit until he was sawed in two. (Martyrdom and Ascension of Isaiah 5:1-14)

As can be heard in reading this story, the storyteller is first of all asking the listeners to sympathize with and revere Isaiah as a true prophet of Israel. But the narrator also asks them to recognize the great wrong that was done by Belkira, Manasseh, the false prophets, and the people. The story appeals to the listeners to change their minds in relation to Isaiah and the issues for which he died. It also implicitly asks the listeners to separate themselves from Belkira and Manasseh and the positions they represented. Thus, both the storyteller and the audience are assumed to be Jews. This is Jewish polemic against other Jewish groups.

The same dynamics are present in this episode of the story of Jesus' death. The shock of the story is that the people and the leaders of *our* religion treat Jesus in this manner. Clearly the storyteller's attitude is highly critical of the chief priests, the scribes, and the people. But the storyteller's attitude is not anti-Jewish. Rather it is a response to the conflict between various Jewish groups. Jesus, his disciples, and those who responded to him were also Jews. Just as in the martyrdom of Isaiah, the story appeals for a highly polarized response of sympathy for Jesus and alienation from other Jews, particularly the chief priests and scribes, who revile him.

The storyteller asks the listeners to recognize *our* corporate involvement in Jesus' death. The crowd was the decisive factor in the reversal of Pilate's offer to release Jesus to his decision to crucify him: "Pilate, wishing to satisfy the crowd . . . " (15:15). In contrast to the Maccabean martyrs who were arrested and tried at the initiative of the Gentiles, Jesus is arrested and handed over to the Gentiles at the initiative of the leaders of Israel. All of the representatives of Israel in the story, from the religious leaders to the people to the condemned criminals, support Jesus' execution and contribute to his derision. That is, Mark appeals to his listeners to recognize that *we* were involved in the death of the Messiah.

The painful irony of Jesus' crucifixion by an alliance between his enemies and his own people is heightened by his cry. It comes at the end of three hours of darkness. The tone of the sentence is dark and foreboding. Once again, the instructions about how the story is to be told are built into the story itself: "with a loud voice" (15:34). Jesus' cry is a recitation of the first line of Psalm 22: " 'Eloi, Eloi lama sabachthani?' which means, 'My God, my God, why have you forsaken me?' " The implication is that Jesus sang this lament of David. It is probable, therefore, that it was also sung as a lament by the storyteller.

Psalm 22 is the song of a righteous sufferer who expresses to

God his feeling of having been abandoned by God. Singing this song did not mean that Jesus had lost faith in God. The psalm is a prayer in which the psalmist first expresses the feelings associated with extreme pain, then describes the horror of his situation, and finally promises to praise God in the congregation upon his recovery. Thus, Jesus recites a traditional prayer of a righteous Jew who is near death.

The episode ends with the storyteller's translation of the prayer from Aramaic into Greek. Again, the narrator directly addresses his listeners. The effect of this repetition of Jesus' words is similar to the two descriptions of the crucifixion (15:24-25). The first makes present the event as it actually happened in the past, through the chanting of Jesus' words. The translation is given in the context of the storyteller's present relationship with his audience.

The bystanders misunderstand Jesus' words. The words *Eloi* and *Eliyah* have similar sounds, particularly in Aramaic. In popular Jewish legend, Elijah was expected to come to the rescue of the godly in time of need. And, just as people laugh at legendary superstitions such as Santa Claus now, the implication is that these bystanders either deliberately misconstrued Jesus' cry or laughed at what they perceived to be his last-ditch appeal to naïve belief.

The final blow of humiliation and undeserved mockery is the offering of the sour wine (or vinegar). The gesture of this one bystander appears, at first, to be a gesture of kindness. Thirst was a major cause of death by crucifixion. But his words make clear his motivation. A little sour wine might keep Jesus alive a little longer. They don't expect Elijah but they can prolong the mocking. The offer of the wine is only a way to continue their fun. What appears at first to be a sympathetic gesture turns out to be the final twist of disdain. The sentence that describes Jesus' death is introduced by the phrase "But Jesus." This adversative conjunction implies that Jesus did not drink the sour wine but kept his vow of abstinence to the end. His response to this final act of spite against him is to cry out and die.

The final episode reports three responses to Jesus' death—by God, the centurion, and the women. God's response is the rending of the curtain of the Temple. In the telling of the story, this is a response of grief. The implied gesture is the rending of the garments. This action by God is the first sympathetic response to Jesus' suffering since the carrying of his cross by Simon of Cyrene. God had not forsaken Jesus.

The centurion's response is, first of all, respect and honor. His words are introduced by a description of his perspective "opposite" Jesus. The introduction is a time in the story in which the listeners can look at the cross from the centurion's point of view. His statement is an even more graphic reversal of expectations than that of the one who offered Jesus the sour wine. The expectation is that he will be hostile and mock Jesus. That is the pattern of Roman response to Jesus that has been established in the Pilate trial and the mockery by the soldiers. His words are then a surprise. This Gentile executioner even uses the title "Son of God," which has been used extensively earlier in the story (Mark 1:11; 3:11; 5:7; 9:7).

The climax of the episode is the description of the women who were watching (15:40-41). It is a long narrative comment that describes the relationship between these women and Jesus. The list of the three names is long. Only the names associated with one of the women, "*Mary* the mother of *James* the younger and *Joses*," have been used earlier in the narrative. In the story of Jesus' rejection at Nazareth, the Nazarenes say, "Isn't this . . . the son of *Mary* and brother of *James* and *Joses* and Judas and Simon?" (Mark 6:3). These are the only instances of these names prior to this description. The verbal thread, therefore, implies that this woman was Jesus' mother. The phrase "James, the younger" is an abbreviation of "James, the younger brother." The threads, traced back through the narrative tapestry, are subtly interwoven with this earlier story of Jesus in Nazareth and with the story of the seven brothers and their mother in the Maccabean tradition. But, for anyone who knew those stories, the connections were unmistakable.

Thus, the storyteller, with his characteristic indirectness, describes the women who mourned for Jesus as he died. Their grief and mourning is only implied. The climax of the story of Jesus' death is the description of these three women to whom he was close and a group of other women who had traveled to Jerusalem with him.

Connections

The primal connections of our experience with this story are experiences of consciousness and confession of personal and corporate sinfulness and experiences of abandonment in suffering and death. These correspond to primary dimensions of Jesus' role in this story. On the cross, Jesus, the Christ, suffers the results of our personal and corporate actions of sinful rebellion and hostility toward God. But Jesus is also a human being on the cross, who experiences the suffering of all of humanity and who, in the midst of that suffering, feels abandoned by God. In prayer, group discussion, and corporate worship, these connections with the story of Jesus' crucifixion and death can be explored as a means of discerning the intersections of our stories with God's story.

The foremost connection with this story is awareness of human captivity to the powers of sin and death. The season of Lent, the observance of Holy Week and especially of Good Friday, the stations of the cross, and the last meditations of the family rosary are Christian traditions that have enabled men and women to explore these connections with the story. The awareness of our personal responsibility for Jesus' suffering and death has led to the examination of conscience and to repentance. The sense of guilt and grief that is often an aspect of these meditations continues the spirit that is present in the story itself. These are then appropriate connections with this memory.

However, our traditions of meditation on Jesus' death have often centered almost exclusively on the awareness of personal sin. The story, on the other hand, concentrates on the sinfulness of human communities, such as the nation and the religion. While the failure of the disciples and Peter is a principal motif in the story, the crucifixion story focuses on the hostile actions of the crowd, the soldiers, and the religious leaders as groups in Jesus' death. The story appeals to its listeners to recognize our involvement with the atrocities of these groups against Jesus.

The story invites us, therefore, to explore the relationships between our involvement with corporate powers of sin and death and this narrative of human rebellion and hostility toward Jesus Christ. A way of opening ourselves to this dimension of the tradition is to identify the ways in which the groups with which we are identified are involved in sin against God and other people. That is, the story invites us to meditate on our involvement in the forces that cause war, racial oppression, starvation, sexual abuse, and poverty. A way of listening for these connections is to identify—in prayer, with another person, or in corporate worship—a communal situation in which you are involved and then to listen to the account of Jesus' crucifixion and death in that context. In contrast to the sense of despair and helplessness that meditation on these cosmic powers so often produces, the story itself may guide us to an appropriate awareness of both our particular involvement and our potential for change.

One of the most graphic stories I have ever heard that connects with this dimension of the crucifixion story was told by a Jewish woman at a predominantly Christian gathering. As I remember the event, she read a document that was discovered in Latvia after World War II. It was written by a young boy. I will recount this story on the basis of notes I took while it was being read.

On the eve of Rosh Hashanna in 1941, the entire Jewish community of our town was gathered together and we were all confined to the synagogue without water, food, or relief for forty-eight hours. They brought lunatics from the asylum to guard us. The week before our rabbi had addressed our congregation and told us that imminent destruction was present for all of us and argued that we should fight, that we would indeed die, but that we would die with honor. The community took a vote and the majority of the community refused. And so we waited.

After those two days, we were led out of town; the

rabbi led us. We were taken in groups of about 250 out to the Jewish cemetery past the edge of town. There, we were all made to take off our clothes, and to line up along a ditch that they had dug. Then one by one they shot each of us in the back of the neck. I was standing beside my father, and he was holding me by the hand. I timed the shots and listened to the rhythm of it.

When they came to me, at the instant when the shot went off I fell into the trench and it went over my head. Then one by one the others fell on top of me, my father and my uncle. The shooting went on for hours and more and more people fell on top of me until I was afraid I was going to suffocate. Finally, after many hours, the shooting stopped. They threw some dirt over the bodies and they went away.

After some hours, I managed to get out. Naked, cold, and covered with blood, I went to some homes that were nearby on the edge of the village along the road out to the cemetery. These were homes of Christians and I hoped that one of them would save me. I knocked on the first door and a peasant came to the door and looked at me and said, "You're a Jew. Go back to the grave where you belong."

I went on to the next house, knocked on the door and again, Christians came to the door. I pleaded with them, but they said, "Go back to your people, Jew. Join them. Stay with them." I went to all those doors and none of them would help me.

Finally, I remembered a widow who lived nearby whom I had known slightly, and I thought "Surely she will help me; she is a good Christian woman." And I went to the home of the widow and knocked on the door. She looked at me and she said, "I know you. You are one of the Jews. Go to the Jews. Go to the grave with your people." I begged her. She said, "Go to your own people. No one will help you here."

I went away and in a short time came back to the house, and knocked again. This time I said, "I am not who you thought. I am Jesus Christ, who has come back. I am broken, bleeding, and I need your help. I have come to you." She fell at my feet. She wiped my feet and begged me to come in. She cleaned me up, put clothes on me and fed me. I said, "You must say nothing about my visit to anyone for it is only to you that I have come." She gave me food, clothes, and after I had rested, I went over again how I had come only to her and that she was to say nothing. Then I went out into the forest and joined the partisans and organized what became the Jewish resistance in Latvia.

In listening to this story against the background of the story of Jesus' death, the appropriateness of its dynamics is crystal clear. Christian anti-Semitism was a part of the forces that led to this particular event and to the Holocaust. Confession, grief, and repentance are an appropriate response for Christians to this story. The person who read this document to us appealed to us as Christians to recognize Christian involvement in the Holocaust. In a similar manner, Mark told the story of Jesus' crucifixion as an appeal for both Jews and Gentiles to recognize their involvement in Jesus' death. That is, there are profound connections between the dynamics of these two stories. Hearing the story of this survivor of the Holocaust may help us to understand some of the impact of the story of Jesus' crucifixion and death in its original context. So also, Jesus' story may shed light on the meaning of the Holocaust.

The other primal connection with this story is with Jesus as a human being who suffers as we do. There is a deep congruence between Jesus' feeling of being abandoned by God on the cross and our experience of suffering and death. Part of the power of this story is that Jesus, as both a human being and as God, experienced the most extreme suffering and humiliation in his death. For every person who experiences extreme suffering and humiliation, this story is a potential place of profound intersection with God's story.

The most accurate way that I can describe my understanding of this connection is to tell you a story from my own experience.

Telling about the gift of this story to me in a time of crisis may help to clarify the ways in which God may be present to others through this story.

As I have recounted earlier, in early November of 1974, November ninth to be exact, I was hit by a car in a service station on the Bronx River Parkway in New York. I had been standing in back of a car waiting to speak to the attendant when another car came off the parkway and was unable to stop. Both of my legs and knees were fractured. Two inches of my right leg were smashed and my knee was punctured from the back through to the front.

Because of the danger of infection, I was given heavy antibiotics, which saved my legs. But by Thanksgiving, almost three weeks later, I had developed colitis and was able to take only fluids. My roommate, who had supported me during those weeks, had left the day before. Friends and family had come to the hospital that day. But they were at home eating together and I was in the hospital.

That night, I became very depressed. I watched a football game in the evening and realized I would never play again—not just football but any sports. And then I watched a war movie. That was even more depressing. I felt totally overwhelmed by the powers of darkness and death. About 2:00 in the morning, the pain became very severe. When I rang the bell for a pain shot, the night nurse refused to come. The battle of the bell went on and on. By 3:30 I was so depressed and the pain was so severe, I wanted to die. For the first time in my life, I wished I could die. I was all alone; the door was closed. And I began to yell as loud as I could in total frustration: "Why? Why have you let this happen to me? My God, my God, why have you forsaken me? Why have you left me alone like this? Why?"

When I realized what I was saying, I found myself remembering the story and just going on with the words. It was not at all difficult for me to identify those who were standing there at the foot of the cross. My nurse fit right into that role! I could see her laughing at me: "Let's see who will come and give him a pain shot!" I went over and over the story in my mind: the crucifixion, the mockery, the darkness and the cry, his death, and those who were watching. And the more I told it, the less I was alone. I had a companion who understood what I was going through, who had suffered for me.

And, when I thought about my situation in relation to Jesus' situation, it became clear that I was in pretty good shape. I started doing a detailed comparison of my condition with his: "This nurse is a rat but eventually she is going to come; Jesus had no one to give him a pain shot. I am in a bed; he was on a cross. I am in pain; he was in pain. But he was dying; I am not going to die. He was publicly exposed; I am in a hospital bed and people are caring for me. He was ridiculed and mocked by everyone; this nurse is taunting me but I have a lot of wonderful nurses who care for me and respect me. I am here because of a stupid accident; he chose to be there so that I would know God is with me. He chose to be there for me so that I would never be alone, no matter how bad it gets."

And the more I remembered, the more my situation improved. I had a comrade in suffering. I was no longer alone. Remembering the story was the means by which Jesus Christ was present with me in that hour of depression and pain. It transformed the context in which I experienced the pain. And it was the turning point in my recovery. I stopped being an innocent victim who felt like I was being attacked by God and became a responsible agent in my own recovery. I started thinking about the resurrection possibilities in my situation, about the ways that God might be able to make something good out of this mess.

In a direct sense, this experience was the beginning of this book and of the recovery of biblical storytelling. I had been performing the stories and people had found them entertaining. But it changed no one's life. As I reflected on this experience, it became clear why. Only those things that I had internalized were available to me in the times of deepest stress. I needed to find a way to enable others to internalize the stories deeply. In a unique way, God can be present through the stories, the psalms, and the prayers that become a part of our interior selves. This realization was the beginning of the search to make the stories available to others, of which this book is an integral part.

Telling the Story

The story of Jesus' death is told in the life of the Church each Holy Week, in particular on Good Friday. These recitals are a steady reinforcement of our communal memory. Furthermore, each time that we celebrate the Eucharist we remember Christ's death. The telling of this story can happen in many different personal and community contexts. But most people never learn the stories so that they can tell them either to themselves or to others. There are a variety of ways in which this can be encouraged.

The following story describes one way in which the liturgical recital of the passion narrative can become an important dimension of a community's life. Richard Rice, presently the director of the Methodist City Society in New York, is the teller of this tale. When he was a pastor in Brooklyn, he found that enabling the men and women of his congregation to tell the passion/resurrection narrative was both a meaningful lay education experience and an enrichment of Lenten worship. This is the story of their experience:

Our group began meeting about eight weeks before Easter. After the first meetings, we agreed that one person in the group would learn the story and tell it in worship for the Scripture lesson each week during Lent. This became a primary focus of the group's life as we helped each person get ready to tell the story the next week and then celebrated their victory in actually doing it.

The response of the congregation to the telling of the stories was extremely positive, which provided a high degree of incentive for the group. People were excited to see other lay persons telling the stories from memory. They also found the lessons more alive which in turn helped my preaching. About halfway through Lent, I realized that the group was also learning a great deal about the passion and resurrection narrative in Mark. But the success of this as a biblical study group was almost incidental to the contribution the group was making to the worship services of the congregation.

Sometime around the middle of Lent, I proposed to the group that we would tell the entire passion narrative for the Good Friday service. At first, people were reluctant and thoroughly frightened. But when I made it clear that they would only have to tell the stories they had already learned and I would do the rest, they were finally more than willing to do it.

On Good Friday, we rearranged the pews so that the congregation was gathered around us in a rough semi-circle with the group seated on a bench facing them. We began by singing two passion hymns and then we simply told the story. There were two other hymns during the telling of the story. As the story progressed, the congregation became more and more deeply involved. By the end there was a primary sense of the holiness and the reality of Jesus' death. It was the most meaningful Good Friday service we have ever had. The people were so appreciative and asked that we tell the story every year.

This experience has made me aware of the power of the story when it is simply told. No sermon could have been more powerful than that story. And the people who told the story have become far more committed leaders in the life of the congregation. Telling the story changed them. It is clear to me that telling the biblical stories introduces a whole new element of meaning that has simply not been present before in the way we have used the Scriptures.

10

RESURRECTION

(Mark 16:1-8)

The story of Jesus' resurrection sets the shame, defeat, and injustice of the crucifixion in the context of the glory, victory, and justice of the new age of the kingdom of God. Having experienced Jesus' death and burial from the perspective of the women, listeners are invited to join them on their trip to the tomb where they find a young man quietly announcing Jesus' resurrection. The story ends with the commission of the women to tell the story of Jesus' resurrection. The final reversal in the story, as Mark recounts it, is the women's response of flight and silence. Their response to the commission is both completely understandable and utterly wrong. The story invites listeners to be open to the purging of their fear in response to this commission.

In the earlier stories, I have preserved with very minor changes the Revised Standard Version translation of the Greek text. In this story, however, the meaning and impact of the story is intimately related to verbal threads that are not preserved in the Revised Standard Version translation. For this reason, it is necessary to give a translation for storytelling that renders those verbal threads in English.

179

The Story

And when the sabbath was past, Mary Magdalene, and
Mary the mother of James, and Salome bought
spices, so that they might go and anoint him.
And very early on the first day of the week they went out
to the tomb, as the sun was rising.

☆　☆　☆　☆　☆

And they were saying to one another, "Who will roll away
the stone for us from the door of the tomb?"
And looking up, they saw that the stone was rolled back.
For it was very large.

☆　☆　☆　☆　☆

And going into the tomb, they saw a young man sitting on
the right hand, clothed in a white robe, and they were
amazed.
And he said to them, "Do not be amazed.

☆　☆　☆　☆　☆

You seek Jesus of Nazareth, who was crucified.
He has been raised.

☆　☆　☆　☆　☆

He is not here.
See the place where they laid him.

☆　☆　☆　☆　☆

But go, tell his disciples and Peter that he is going before
you to Galilee.
There you will see him, as he told you."

☆　☆　☆　☆　☆

And going out from the tomb, the women fled.
For trembling and astonishment had come upon them.

☆　☆　☆　☆　☆

And they told nothing to any one.
For they were afraid.

Learning the Story

Verbal Threads

"The tomb." The story is structured around the women's relationship to the tomb: "They went to the tomb" (vs. 2); "And going into the tomb" (vs. 5), "And going out of the tomb" (vs. 8). This verbal thread, which introduces each of the movements in the women's trip to the tomb, is the primary link between the parts of the story.

"The stone." The stone episode is organized around this verbal thread: "Who will roll away the stone" (vs. 3); "the stone was rolled back" (vs. 4). This verbal thread picks up the motif at the end of the burial story of Joseph rolling the stone over the door of the tomb (15:46).

"Amazed." The climax of the description of what the women saw in the tomb is that they were amazed (vs. 5). The English word is a poor substitute for the Greek *(ekthambeomai)*, which has connotations of both terror and wonder. It is a highly emotional word that captures the full range of their emotions: amazement, terror, wonder. The young man's response is a word of calm: "Do not be amazed" (vs. 6). This verbal thread is the objective correlative of this initial interaction between the women and the young man, which moves from panic to not-panic.

"Go and tell"/"they told nothing." The usual English translation, "they said nothing," does not preserve the verbal links of the original narrative, therefore the change here. The conflict between the young man's command and the women's response is concretized in this verbal thread. The young man says, "Go and tell the disciples and Peter"; the women "told nothing to anyone" (vss. 6, 8).

"For." The last two episodes conclude with two climactically short sentences that share a common key word, "for" (vs. 8*b*, *d*). This conjunction (in Greek, *gar*) is consistently used by Mark to introduce narrative comments. These narrative comments explain why the women fled from the tomb ("For trembling and astonishment had come upon them") and why they told no one anything ("For they were afraid"). This one-word verbal thread ties these two climactic episodes together.

The young man's announcement to the women is the most complex part of the story and the most difficult to learn. The structure is straightforward and, once recognized, is easy to remember. The first episode has the theme of amazement. The second is organized on the antinomy of crucifixion and resurrection: "Jesus who was crucified"/"He has been raised." The third addresses the evidence of the resurrection: his absence and the command to look at the place where he had been laid. The fourth is the commission to go and tell and the promise of Jesus' appearance to them.

Listening to the Story

This story has an unprecedented number of short sentences. This indicates the tempo at which the story was told. The story goes from moderato to slow to very slow. It is in musical terms a long and steady retard. The short sentences are each given a full breath. As a result, the story gradually slows down to a climax of joyful intensity and poignant mystery.

The time is the story's first note. "When the sabbath was past" means Saturday evening after sundown. "Very early on the first day of the week" means Sunday morning. Just as the listener can count Peter's three denials (14:68, 70-71), so also here the listener can count the days: sabbath, the day after sabbath. Add these days to the reference to the day before sabbath, the day in which the burial took place (15:42), and the total is three days. The possibility of the fulfillment of Jesus' prophecy of resurrection on the third day (8:31; 9:31; 10:34) is thereby subtly introduced. It is interesting that the fulfillment of both this prophecy and the prophecy of Peter's denial is confirmed in the narrative by inviting the listener to count in threes (see 14:66-71).

The recital of the women's names recalls their presence at Jesus' death and burial and their faithfulness to him both in Galilee and in his moment of greatest need. This repetition of their names also reinforces the listener's positive identification with the women and their grief. Of all the followers of Jesus, only the women were present at his death to mourn for him.

The episode of the trip to the tomb ends with another allusion to the dawning of a new time. Ever since the deep darkness that introduced the recounting of Jesus' death (15:33), the atmosphere of the story itself has been darkness and gloom. The burial was on Friday evening just before dark, and the women bought spices Saturday night after dark (16:1). This night imagery is a clue to the tone of the storyteller. Everything is darkness and death. The trip to the tomb begins in the darkness of the early morning, but it ends in the light—"as the sun was rising" (vs. 2).

The stone episode intensifies the identification with the women. The report of the women's question is the first direct expression of their grief (vs. 3). The content of their question is factual but the emotions implied in their words are grief and sorrow.

The discovery of the stone rolled back is described through the women's eyes: "And looking up, they saw" (vs. 4). The narrator's tone is surprise and shock. The amazement of the women thereby expressed is explained in the concluding comment to the listeners: "For it was very large" (vs. 4b, author's trans.). Here Mark explains why the women were so stunned that the stone had been rolled back.

The entry into the tomb has the haunting tone of ghost stories and descriptions of the place of the dead. The discovery of the young man is once again reported from the women's point of view: "And going into the tomb, they saw" (vs. 5). The surprise of what they saw is related to the motifs in the story it picks up:

And a *young man* followed him *clothed in* a linen cloth over his nakedness. (14:51—the climax of the flight of the disciples at the arrest)

And you will see the Son of Man *seated on the right hand* of Power, and coming with the clouds of heaven. (14:62—Jesus' messianic confession to the high priest)

And going into the tomb, they saw a *young man seated on the right hand, clothed in* a white robe and they were amazed. (16:5)

Earlier in the story, the image of a young man clothed in a linen garment symbolizes the shame of the flight of the disciples. The image is here reversed into a symbol of divine presence, a young man clothed in a white robe. Furthermore, his being seated on the right hand is verbally connected with the Son of man's position of power. This image characterizes the young man as a divine messenger who stands near the throne of God.

The storyteller's description of the amazement and alarm of the women is the first explicit insight into the women's emotions. Until now in the story, their emotions had to be inferred from the narrator's tone. This direct description of their alarm creates a strong sympathetic identification with the women.

The young man first calms their fears. As we have seen in the angel's response to the shepherds, this is in the best tradition of angels in New Testament narratives (Luke 2:10; also 1:29-30).

The young man's reference to Jesus as the one who was crucified recalls the shame of Jesus' execution. It would be similar to describing someone as "Jesus, who was executed in an electric chair." The announcement of the resurrection is only one word in Greek, *agertha,* which means "He has been raised." The passive tense indicates that this was an action of God. This one word, spoken in a soft and calm voice, is the supreme fulfillment of Jesus' passion and resurrection prophecies and the confirmation that Jesus is the Messiah.

The evidence of the resurrection is the empty tomb. The young man's pointing to the place where Jesus was laid refers back to the climax of the burial episode:

Mary Magdalene and Mary the mother of Joses *saw where he was laid.* (15:47)

See the place *where they laid him.* (16:6d)

Again, the words that were the sign of defeat are transformed into the sign of victory. And, because of the number of times the storyteller has described what the women saw, it is possible here for the listeners to visualize that empty tomb.

The young man commissions the women to go and tell (vs. 7). The message the women are to tell the disciples is a paraphrase of Jesus' earlier promise to the disciples:

But after I have been raised, I will go *before you into Galilee*. (14:28)

He is *going before you into Galilee*. (16:7)

The young man's message concludes with the promise of an appearance. Furthermore, in the aftermath of the disciples' flight and Peter's denial, his message holds out the promise of reconciliation with Jesus. The final emphasis is on the fulfillment of Jesus' prophecies "just as he said to you" (vs. 7). The young man's tone in this climactic commission is full of joy and energy.

The plot of the entire Gospel here reaches its conclusion. The prophecies of Jesus are being fulfilled. Many more remain to be fulfilled, but the fulfillment of the resurrection prophecy makes the fulfillment of the others certain. The resurrection confirms Jesus' status as both a true prophet and as the Messiah. The earlier signs of defeat in his passion and death are now transformed into signs of victory. The expectation of condemnation for the disciples and Peter is changed into the promise of reconciliation. The place of grief in the tomb is now a place of joy. The humiliation of a young man's naked flight is changed into the glory of a young man in a white robe seated at the right hand. Jesus' way of suffering and death, which seemed so absurd, has been confirmed as the road to victory. In light of the resurrection, everything is turned around. Thus, the effect of the young man's announcement to the women is to transform the causes of grief into reasons for joy. But it is all done in a very restrained manner.

The flight of the women is, therefore, a total reversal of expectations (vs. 8). The associations of the word for "flight" *(pheugo)* were determined earlier by its use to describe the flight of the disciples and the young man (14:50, 52). The narrator explains the flight of the women by describing their extreme emotions: "trembling, quivering" *(tromos)*, and "astonishment, terror" *(ekstasis)*. This narrative comment is an intimate explanation of their action. It implies that the storyteller regarded their action as wrong. Their flight must be explained. And yet it is given with such emotional intensity that the listeners can understand and even sympathize with the women's response.

The women's silence is even more incredible than their flight. It is in direct contradiction to the angel's command. The story they are commissioned to tell is joyful good news. Why would they tell nothing to anyone? The narrator's explanation is a climactic two-word sentence in Greek, *ephobounto gar,* which means "for they were afraid" (vs. 8). Once again, this narrative explanation is an intimate insight into the women's inner motives. Thus, the sympathetic identification with the women is maintained at the same time that the shock of their disobedience to the angel's command is explained.

Why would they be afraid? In the context in which the story was originally told, there are a range of explanations: fear as a response to being in the presence of God, the possibility of persecution due to association with a crucified man, the potential for mockery since women were considered unreliable witnesses, and the unprecedented character of this commission for women. Fear as holy awe is a frequent response to being in the presence of God in the biblical tradition. From the man in the garden (Gen. 3:10), to Moses at the burning bush (Exod. 3:4-6), to the death of Uzzah when he touched the ark (II Sam. 6:6-7), fear is an appropriate response to being in the presence of God or one of God's messengers (for example, Baalam and his perceptive ass, Num. 22:21-35). In Mark, people frequently respond with fear to the actions of Jesus: the disciples at Jesus' calming of the sea (4:41); the crowd at Jesus' healing of the demoniac (5:15); the woman who was healed from a flow of blood when Jesus called her (5:33); the disciples seeing Jesus walking on the water (6:50). These are presented as appropriate and right responses. Thus, the women's fear is a fully understandable response to what they heard and saw in the tomb.

For Mark's listeners, the possibility of persecution and ostracism for those who would tell the Jesus story was real. After all, in the story itself, the young man was seized in the garden and Peter barely avoided being arrested and condemned with Jesus. Jesus was executed as a criminal. The persecution of Christians by other Jews was not usually violent. But the attacks on Stephen and Paul (Acts 6–7, 21–23) were probably part of the common memory. And Christians were increasingly ostracized from the Jewish community in the period after the Jewish war, as the Pharisees pursued their policy of centralization. Roman persecution was also a growing threat in the aftermath of the Jewish war. Christians had been blamed by Nero for the fire in Rome in A.D. 64, and hundreds were killed. The persecution of Christians under Domitian (A.D. 93–96) was the culmination of hostility toward Christians during the Roman administrations of the New Testament period. For Mark's listeners, therefore, the commission to go and tell the stories of Jesus' resurrection was related to the possibility of taking up your own cross. Being publicly identified with Jesus was potentially dangerous.

Finally, this commission to the women is a major reversal of the roles of men and women in the tradition of Israel. Generally, men rather than women were called by divine messengers to be the agents who would announce the actions of God. With the exception of Deborah, men, from Moses through the prophets, were called to deliver God's messages to the people. Furthermore, in the earlier parts of the Gospel, women are neither mentioned as disciples nor are they called by Jesus to take roles of leadership. Therefore, the commission to deliver this most critical message is a total reversal of normal expectations for women. For the listeners, a response of fear by the women would be fully understandable. Not only are the women inadequately prepared but also a hostile or skeptical response is probable if they *do* attempt to carry out the commission. Such a commission for women was utterly unexpected and would have been highly controversial.

of the women's silence, the fact remains that in the story their silence is radically wrong. They have the best and most important news that anyone has ever been given to tell. Their silence is the ultimate irony. Earlier in the Gospel, the leper and the people in the Decapolis who were commanded to be silent ran out and proclaimed the news (1:45; 7:36). Here those who are commanded to proclaim even greater good news are silent.

The effect of this ending is to open up a whole new plot: the story of the mission of the church. A whole new mystery is thus introduced. The story leaves the listeners with a major puzzle: will the story be told? Obviously, as the telling of the story itself demonstrates, the women had told the story of what they saw and heard. But, to whatever degree the listeners identify with the women's fear, the question about whether the story will be told is a question they must ask themselves. The story requires that every listener reflect about the response of running away from this commission and remaining silent. The story's implicit appeal is to go and tell the story regardless of trembling, terror, and fear. In the end, therefore, it is up to the listeners to determine how the story will end.

Telling this supremely mysterious ending requires the storyteller to honor the profound silence with which the story ends. To lead the listeners into this silence is to invite them to meditate on the wonder and mystery of the resurrection and the awesome commission that it entails.

Connections

The connections that make a vital telling of this story possible begin with the experiences of darkness, of the times when the powers of sin and death seem to be totally dominant. These are the times of grief, helplessness, devastation, and awareness of our personal and corporate captivity. That is where the story of the resurrection begins, with the women who loved Jesus, preparing to go out to the tomb to love him for the last time. These are times of letting go of loved ones and loved projects. They are times of abandonment, of giving up hopes and dreams.

Thus, these experiences of the dark night are a context in

which to hear the story. In a group, it is appropriate to ask persons to share them with a spiritual companion. A form of the question is, in what ways do you now feel subject to the power of sin and death? How are you presently in the dark night of death? This is one way by which we can connect with the experience of the women going to the tomb.

It is in the midst of these dark nights that the clues, intimations, and realities of Jesus' resurrection can happen. The deepest power of this story is to open our eyes to see and our ears to hear the signs of the victory of the powers of the new age of God's kingdom. It calls our attention to the ways in which God transforms death into life. The story is itself the sign that the victory has been won in Jesus' resurrection.

In this story, as in the birth narrative, the foremost problem is how to bring authenticity to the words of a divine messenger. Identifying with the women's experience of grief and despair is relatively easy. Presenting an angel's report of the decisive victory in the cosmic struggle between the powers of good and evil is more difficult. We do not have as many points of connection with that message. As in the birth narrative, the young man's report is related to experiences of telling unexpected good news to someone. However, the announcement of the resurrection has a depth of quiet and mystery that is different from the birth narrative. The joy and mystery of this story is absolutely unique.

The dominant underlying spirit of this narrative is peace and wonder. Rather than a victory celebration with fireworks and brass bands, this cosmic victory is celebrated in the quiet of a tomb. But, rather than talk about this spirit of the resurrection story, let me tell you a story about it.

When I returned to teaching the year after the accident, I decided to teach a course about the resurrection. After the experience of nearly dying and in the midst of the ongoing struggle to recover, I wanted to understand more about the resurrection. And so I did what teachers often do. If you want to learn about something, teach a course about it. And this was my plan: we would memorize and tell all of the resurrection narratives. We would study them in detail and through telling the stories we would seek to experience the resurrection of Christ. I wanted to find the spirit of the resurrection.

I assumed that if we really experienced the resurrection, if we in some sense found it, we would experience great ecstasy and joy. It would be like the ultimate Easter: trumpets blasting, hymns of joy and triumph, lilies everywhere, people hugging. We would all be ecstatic. And I hoped for that kind of ecstasy.

Somewhat to my surprise, ten people were interested in studying the resurrection. And we did it all: we studied, we learned and told the stories, and we searched the Scriptures together. And nothing happened: no ecstasy, no great joy. Nor could I find much of that in the stories. On the last day of class, I proposed that we have an extra session and spend a whole afternoon and evening telling the stories. Maybe if we told the stories all at once, it would happen and I would find some confirmation of my hope.

A woman in the group, Nancy, invited us to her lovely home up in the woods of Connecticut. She and her husband had built it together. But, just as they were finishing that previous spring, he had a heart attack and died. He was only in his mid-forties. Nancy too was on a search to understand and experience the meaning of the resurrection.

We gathered in a room downstairs without any furniture and a big fireplace. I had structured nothing. And so we told some of the stories and sang songs. Then there was a long period of silence. We told more stories, and people began to do some sharing. Nancy shared about her grief and her sense that her husband was still present in the house. We talked about the reality of death and the hope of the resurrection, not a soul living on but a full resurrection of the person.

Then another silence. There were conflicts in the group. There was a black pastor in the group who had been deeply involved in the civil rights movement, and a major conflict emerged between him and two equally militant white feminists in the group. Later, there was a sharp conflict between a more conservative pastor and the liberals in the group. Then more stories and more silence.

We took a break for supper and had communion together. After dishes, we started a fire. More stories, more silence. We told all the resurrection stories. We sang songs. We did lots of sharing. And the silences got longer and deeper. People sat closer together. It was a wonderful, peaceful quiet. But finally, it was time to go.

As we were leaving, I said to them, "Well, it didn't happen. I had hoped that if we told all the stories we would experience the great joy and ecstasy of the resurrection." And they looked at me with surprise, and Nancy said, "But, Tom, don't you understand what has happened? I feel a kind of peace that I have never known before. My husband is gone. But somehow I know he is going to be all right." And, one after another, they began to share what had happened to them in the course and on that day. And they had all had the same kind of experience.

Then it hit me. Peace! That is the spirit of the resurrection. The stories are all quiet. And the spirit of the resurrection stories is a spirit of peace: angels in a tomb with a message; Jesus appearing and saying, "Peace be with you"; conversation and communion on the road to Emmaus. Telling and listening to the stories had made clear the spirit of the mystery of the resurrection and the character of life after death: peace. And the stories had transformed our grief and conflict into a measure of peace and community.

Thus, I would suggest that exploring your experiences of peace will bear fruit in making this story come alive for others. However, the story does not end with peace. The greatest puzzle of Mark's resurrection narrative is the ending.

The principal connection of the ending of Mark's narrative is with the fear of telling the story. A recent study of people's primary fears had a surprising result. The number one fear of more people than any other was *not* nuclear war, cancer, or being a victim of a crime or accident. The number one fear was speaking in public. For most laypersons and many clergy, telling the stories of the Gospels is frightening whether for a large group or for another person.

The possible explanations of the women's silence are points of connection now. One of the major barriers to biblical storytelling is a sense of awe and fear at telling these holy words. Because of the unique associations of these stories with God, I have often felt inadequate. For years, I did not tell the stories because I was afraid I would do it wrong. Thus, in what ways do you feel afraid in the presence of God when you sense the commission to tell these stories? Paying attention to that fear and offering it to God is one way of connecting with the mystery of this story.

The fear that others may misunderstand and be offended by the telling of the stories is real and fully justified. Telling the stories almost inevitably results in conflict and some degree of ridicule or disdain. The reasons are many: hostility toward God, disgust at the negative effects of Christianity in particular or religion in general, anger at the Bible or various schools of biblical interpretation, and sophisticated disdain for the simple-mindedness of merely telling the stories. Some people are simply put off by the mere fact of telling these stories. The richness of the associations of these stories in people's experience is a source of their power. But those associations are often negative as well as positive. And telling the stories calls forth all of those associations. To tell these stories is to be a lightning rod. Thus, the story also invites us to identify and connect to the story our fears of persecution and ridicule. The invitation of the ending is to examine those fears in the perspective of the empty tomb and the commission of the young man.

Finally, there are connections with a sense of inadequacy, of being called to a role for which you have not been prepared. Everyone can identify with the women. Just as Moses felt inadequate to the task, so also each one who is called to tell the stories feels inadequately prepared. The story invites us to identify with the women and the reversal of roles they experienced. In what ways do you feel inadequate and unprepared to tell these stories? What are the sources of your feelings of inferiority? They may be related to your ethnic background, social status, economic class, racial group, sexual identity, or educational background. And each of these dynamics of human communities is experienced in concrete ways rather than in vague generalizations.

The place where I have felt a sense of inadequacy and fear most deeply has been in relation to writing rather than public speaking, and in particular to writing and publishing a book. In the introduction, I recounted the way the idea for this book happened on the journey up the river. But there is more to the story. I first sensed the need for and began to work on this book in 1978. Two years later, I was given a contract for the book and wrote an entire manuscript of over 250 pages over the next two years. The writing was an ordeal for me because of the anxiety and fear that was associated with it. When the manuscript was turned down for publication, I was very discouraged. I tried for another two years to revise it. But the process went nowhere.

At an earlier retreat at the Jesuit Renewal Center, two years before the journey up the river, this quest became a center for my prayers. This retreat was during Holy Week. And on Good Friday afternoon, I told Mark's story of Jesus' passion and death to the community. During that day, I grieved for my father who had died that previous September, and for the book. On the afternoon of Holy Saturday, I went to the nearby Cincinnati Nature Center. The daffodils were in bloom, and it was a beautiful early spring day.

I had my pen with me. My pen was my most precious possession. It was an expensive, red, Parker fountain pen. I had managed to keep it for almost ten years. Every time I lost it, I looked diligently until I found it again. The case was worn from years of use. But it had always worked flawlessly. I loved that pen. It symbolized all of my hopes and dreams of being a writer, a scholar who was respected and famous.

As I walked up a long hill, I sensed from God a call that made absolutely no sense whatsoever. The call was to bury my pen. During this retreat, I had been gifted with such an overwhelming and all-pervasive sense of God's love that there was really no choice but to do it. It was somehow the way in which I was called to join Christ in his death, to abandon what I was holding onto. But it made no sense at all.

I found a place off the path in the midst of a group of daffodils. I dug a little grave with a stick and fashioned a cross out of two small branches to mark the spot. And I buried my pen. I sat and wept for almost an hour, for Dad, for my hopes, for my pen which I really liked, for everything that I had to give up and let go. I left my pen there in the ground.

I sought for months to discern the meaning of this action. For months, I thought it meant to give up writing completely. And I did; for over a year, I wrote nothing. In response to all the questions of friends and associates about the book, which I had announced widely, I could only say, "I have given it up." Only after two years was the idea resurrected, in a whole new form. This book is itself a gift that has grown out of the story of Jesus' death and resurrection. I now see, at least in part, that burying my pen was a way that God could change the associations of writing for me from fear to love.

I know at least something about how the women felt and why they were afraid to tell the stories. Nevertheless, their silence was wrong. The story invites us to explore the mystery of the reasons for saying nothing in light of the commission to go and tell the stories of God's victory.

Telling the Story

In the end, each person is called to tell the story. How will the story of Jesus' death and resurrection end? To tell or not to tell—that is the question with which Mark's story ends.

The commissioning of the women is a clue to the basic strategy for the proclamation of the gospel in early Christianity. The power of the gospel storytelling tradition is in the telling of the stories by the people. The apostles had a crucial public role, as do clergy now. But the gospel as storytelling is not primarily an issue of performances by virtuoso storytellers. There is a vital place for the telling of the stories in public worship and for large gatherings of people. But telling the story is the calling of every follower of Jesus in daily life.

And the calling makes sense. These stories have their greatest impact in the context of the relationships between persons who live and work together. Just as each woman and man has a distinctive storytelling style, so also each of us has a unique network of relationships. The stories of the good news are most meaningful when they are told by one person to another in the context of a personal relationship of care. No one else can tell the stories in the same way. The gospel is made present in the infinitely varied connections between our stories and God's story that can be made by a storytelling network.

If there is one thing I have learned from the past twenty years of studying and telling the stories, it is this: trust the story. The stories of God, when told faithfully out of a commitment to understand and internalize them deeply, have their own power and life. The stories are like the seeds of Jesus' parables. They grow in their own time and in their own way. But they bear fruit far beyond anything one would expect.

This story is told by Louise Mahan, who is pastor of Broadway United Methodist Church in Chicago. It is a story about the way in which the connection between a Gospel story and the life of her congregation was a critical factor in the new life of the community:

I'm the pastor of an inner city church in Chicago, situated a few blocks from Wrigley Field. I became the pastor there in June of 1983, four months after an arsonist burned the building beyond reasonable saving. This was the culmination of two difficult years in the life of the congregation.

We spent the first year I was there fighting with the insurance company and trying to heal wounds, the scars of which will last forever. A rebuilding committee and a rebuilding finance committee were formed and began work. Decisions were made to demolish the old walls and to work with an architect on a new building that would better suit our needs and be handicapped accessible. Pledges were made. But for every small victory, we seemed to suffer two defeats. By the end of the second year, we were all discouraged. The burned out hulk still stood, the insurance settlement was woefully inadequate, we were meeting in a church building where we were only tolerated on Sunday afternoons—the litany of woes could go on and on.

In July of 1985, I attended the first national biblical storytelling festival in Maine. One of the stories we learned was the parable of the sower. Probably because of the allegorical material in the Gospels, I have always, when hearing or reading this story, thought of myself as dirt. I never liked the story much. But as I learned it and told it and told it and heard it told, it suddenly came to me that I was not dirt, but the sower, and that my congregation was filled with sowers! With great excitement, I took the sower back to the people of Broadway UMC.

The first Sunday back we were worshiping on the lawn and I told them the parable. They were immediately engaged by the telling instead of the reading. Then I asked them to line it back to me. They looked at me strangely but I was standing up and they were sitting down so I had some authority, and so they lined it back to me twice.

Then I asked them to tell it to each other. With very little encouragement they did so. Then I preached about our being not dirt but sowers, and that we had been sowing seeds for two years and most had fallen on packed down soil or rocky soil or among thorns, but that some had fallen on good soil and we had seen some results of that and that we would see more results in the future.

We were all encouraged, lifted up, by the story. We used it over and over. It became our story. We used it in worship, on a big banner, at meetings. Every time we got bad news (which was often) someone would tell the story.

We don't need the story much anymore. Our building is going up, and we'll be worshiping in it in the winter of 1987. We'll need a new story for the new people of God that we will be. But I know that without the parable of the sower, Broadway UMC would have disappeared. The story saved us and gave us new life. Thanks be to God!

The telling of the stories of the gospel is a sign of the power of the resurrection of Jesus Christ in the world. But, in the end, the possibility of persons and communities hearing the stories is dependent on one thing: the victory of God's love over the legitimate fears that would prevent each person from telling the stories. No other storyteller can tell the stories in the way that you can.

ENDINGS

A map can be helpful for a journey, especially if it is a journey into new territory. And a principal task of explorers is to make a map for those who want to travel in that new land. This book has been a kind of guide or map for those who want to begin a journey into the gospel as storytelling.

From beginning to end, the author and guide in the background of this journey is Jesus Christ. Jesus is the source of this storytelling tradition. The spirit of Christ continues to be the force behind this storytelling tradition. As we hear and learn these stories by Jesus and about him, we can hear his voice and discern the shape of his character. As we tell the tales, Christ's spirit is present in and through the telling. In this narrative tradition, Jesus Christ tells his own story, first *to* us and then *through* us.

To become a teller of Jesus' tales is to become a disciple of Jesus. As with the pilgrims of Chaucer's *Canterbury Tales,* those who learn these narratives join Jesus and his followers as they travel the roads from Galilee up to Jerusalem. Along the way, we learn his parables and sayings, and we share the things that have happened to us. The story journey means participating in Jesus' journey.

Another dimension of the story journey is that Jesus Christ joins us in our journeys. If the adventures of the Gospels are learned deeply, our stories get woven together with Jesus' story. Jesus becomes a companion, whose words and actions provide a context for the way in which we experience and recount the events of our life journeys. His story becomes a framework for our stories. As things happen, as crises emerge, the memories of his life come up. In ever-new contexts, as we walk along, Jesus appears out of the shadows and reminds us of an event or a saying that sets our experiences in a new light. Just as with the two on the road to Emmaus (Luke 24:13-32), Jesus becomes a storyteller companion who is traveling our way.

The life journey becomes a series of interconnecting stories. Christ's story and ours are woven together. The events of our lives are the episodes of an ongoing narrative that is given meaning and perspective by Jesus. Our stories find their source and their destiny in being linked with his. In turn, the gospel tradition is given fresh meaning by being connected with our personal and communal sagas. At the beginning and at the ending of our journeys is Jesus Christ.

The next steps in the journey involve broadening and deepening the connections between God's story and ours. Here are some of the steps that can be taken to explore those relationships.

Study. Learning more about the story and its meaning in its original context is a natural step. This can include anything, from learning about the historical background of Israel and the Hellenistic world of the first century, to studying and even learning the stories in the Greek language, to investigating the theology of the narratives. A way to focus such broader learning is to explore the meaning of a particular story in a general rather than a specific way. This is to study *out* from a gospel narrative into related narratives in the biblical tradition itself and in the traditions of the biblical period.

Potentially, every aspect of the historical-critical study of the Scriptures can be a resource for the story journey. Good critical commentaries on the Gospels are available. The use of diction-aries and concordances broadens and deepens the study of the narratives. The full and unfettered journey of the mind is an integral part of the gospel as storytelling.

Pray. Living into the stories in prayer allows them to become more deeply internalized. *The Spiritual Exercises* of Saint Ignatius of Loyola are a primary resource for this kind of prayer. In the *Exercises,* Ignatius outlines a series of meditations on the life of Christ. They are one way of letting these stories speak to us. Several of the exercises outlined earlier in this book are derived from Ignatius. But an excellent next step would be to do a guided retreat with a director who knows the exercises well.

Master a range of stories. Internalizing a broader range of stories is an obvious next step. There are several ways of selecting the ones to learn next. You might decide to *learn a block of stories,* ranging from a chapter or two of a Gospel to a series of parables or healing stories. Or *learn the passion/resurrection narrative from Mark.* Another possible step is to *learn the stories of the weekly lectionary.* Pastors, teachers, and church members who have done this have found that their weekly worship experience is deepened.

Still another way of mastering a range of stories is to *learn stories that connect with your life story now.* In a period of coping with an illness or stress, you might choose to learn a series of stories about persons who dealt with illness or stress. In each period of individual and congregational life, there are biblical stories that have within them the good news for that period. Meditating upon and choosing the stories, either alone or with a director, is like choosing your own gift at Christmas.

Tell the stories. An essential step in the story journey is to tell the story to someone else. It is best to approach this in stages. Telling the story to another person is a first step. Children are wonderfully receptive story listeners. It is virtually impossible to fail at telling a story to a young child. Whatever you can tell them will be a gift. A trusted friend or a storytelling companion is also a possible first listener. A next step is to tell a story to a small group of two or three persons, perhaps a class that is studying the story. Then telling a story in congregational worship or to someone who really needs to hear a particular story might be the next storytelling adventure.

There is a quantum leap in the story journey when the stories begin to be told to others. It is only in telling someone else that you can experience the resonance and power of the stories through you. To be able to tell good news to someone is a gift. And it will be a gift to your listeners if it is given freely, without pre-determined expectations about its meaning. If you have already decided what the story will mean or ought to mean to someone, don't tell it. Or if you really need for your listeners to respond positively, don't tell it. Only if you can allow your listeners to be free will you ever know what the story can mean to them.

Enable someone else to learn a story. The journey of Christ's story into the world is multiplied when you enable someone else to learn to tell the stories. Whether you do it for one person or a small group, enabling others to become tellers as well as listeners is a good next step. The journey into the gospel as storytelling can be done in an almost infinite variety of ways, depending on the needs of the group. In general, a storytelling process needs to enable persons to take the steps we have taken for each of the stories in this book: learning the story, listening to the story in its original context, connecting with the story in relation to our own experience, and telling the story to someone else. However, this process is like a good jazz melody: there are many good variations that can be played on it. There is no methodological orthodoxy for the story journey. Whatever facilitates the connection between the particular stories of the Gospels and the stories of people's lives will be helpful. And the ways you might use for enabling this to happen will vary with different contexts. Furthermore, you may find something new that no one has ever tried before. As you can see from this report, many people have made distinctive contributions to the exploration of the gospel storytelling tradition. You will know when others have actually been enabled to tell the stories. Seeds will have been sown, and you will see the fruit.

Form or join a storytelling support group. A reality in our time is that storytellers are a little unusual. Therefore, joining with others who are embarking on the same journey is helpful and supportive. There is energy and life in the support that comes from sharing a common task.

The Network of Biblical Storytellers has been formed for precisely this purpose. It is a loosely knit organization of persons who are actively exploring the gospel as storytelling in ministry. There are chapters of the network in several major metropolitan areas of the United States and Canada. The address of the network is included at the end of the bibliography. One of the purposes of the network is to assist persons who want to form or join a group.

While there is a need for such a group now, the time will come when it will no longer be needed. The most natural support groups for the gospel as storytelling are the local church and the seminary. As the storytelling tradition comes alive and is appropriated more generally, the need for a special organization may decrease. At present, however, there is an important role for persons and groups who are called to the task of recovering the gospel as storytelling.

Take on a long-term project of ministry or research. Both individuals and groups can undertake long-term projects of ministry and research. Translations, exegetical commentaries, hermeneutical research, and audio/video materials need to be developed for use in all aspects of ministry. And the biblical storytelling tradition needs to be explored substantively with particular age groups and in relation to the infinite number of special needs that are present.

In any serious effort to explore the gospel's life as an ongoing oral tradition, the relationship between this work and the various disciplines and movements of biblical and theological thought will need to be examined. Historical-critical biblical study, biblical theology, and narrative theology are areas with obvious relationship to this effort. Biblical storytelling also has a major contribution to make to the various aspects of ministry: worship, preaching, pastoral care, religious education, evangelism, missions, world religions, ecumenics, and church administration.

The gospel as storytelling is a primary language of the Church. Story, song, poetry, prophecy, law, liturgy, and wisdom sayings are the primary forms and languages of the religion of Israel. Secondary languages are used to reflect upon our use of the primary languages. Theology, philosophy of religion, and history are the major secondary languages of our tradition. The vitality of the secondary languages and their disciplines is dependent upon the richness and depth of the primary languages. Story is the most important of the primary languages of the Church, and the stories of Jesus Christ are the most central stories. The gospel as storytelling is certainly not the only means for the revitalization of the Church's life and mission, but it is a central one.

Telling the Gospel stories is a way in which we can be sensitized to Jesus Christ's presence among us. As in the Eucharist, the real presence of Jesus Christ can be perceived and known in the faithful telling of the stories of the Gospels. Wherever the Gospel narratives are faithfully told, the living Christ will be present there in the midst of them.

I sense that the living Christ is calling those who would join this story journey to a distinctive discipleship in our time. A major challenge that lies before us is to integrate the world of electronic media into the Church's ongoing mission of proclamation in word and deed. An approach to this task is implicit in recognizing the mutually complementary relationship between the gospel as storytelling and the gospel as text. I used to think that this relationship was, to some degree, contradictory, but I have changed my mind. While there are differences that need to be recognized, story and text are mutually dependent. The storytelling of the community of Israel gave birth to the biblical texts. And the texts of the Scriptures have, in different ways, led to the recovery of telling the stories. Now, in turn, the telling of the stories is bearing fruit in new texts. And these texts will generate more storytelling. In a similar manner, the gospel in electronic media will both grow out of and give life to the gospel in story and text.

We are called to tell the stories of God, who is known in the life of Israel and in Jesus Christ. What becomes of them is up to God. In an electronic age in which storytelling is once again becoming a primary language of communication in the emerging global village, the gospel as storytelling may be one of the means God will choose to make known Jesus Christ's victory over the powers of sin and death.

Appendix

NARRATIVE ANALYSIS WORKSHEET

Kenneth R. Parker

This worksheet is a guide for "translating" a Biblical narrative text from a writing-and-reading medium to a telling-and-listening medium. It is organized around four qualitative components found in Aristotle's *Poetics:* plot, character, thought, and diction.

1. *Plot* is the structure of the story's action expressed as a decisive transaction, struggle, or change with assessable consequences in a life. It is the human action of the story. Analysis of plot proceeds in two directions.

   A. *Structure:* Try to discern the overall sequence of events within which the story is placed. With biblical stories, how are things being built up and pulled together? What is the impact of this story upon that? Look at the book as a whole and at the section of the book in which the story occurs.

   Next try to discern internal structure of events through which the story is developed. What signs of tensions and resolutions are there? What is the impact of all this upon the storylisteners?

   tensions: *resolutions:*

B. *Episodes:* Identify the steps in the story. These steps are usually two, three, or four sentence episodes, each of which deals with a common subject matter. When the who's, what's, where's, when's and how's change, chances are a new episode has begun. Watch for possible structural parallelisms between the first and last episodes. Name each episode in a way that will trigger your memory concerning its contents.

2. *Character* is the motivation of the story's characters by which they are ascribed moral qualities on the basis of what they seek or avoid. It is the human motivation of the story. Analysis of character proceeds in three directions.

A. *Perspective:* Notice the shifts from "objective" description of the story's action to "subjective" interpretation of the story's characters. These inside points of view are rarely used, but when they are, they give insights into the characters that are invaluable to a person trying to "get into" the story.

B. *Norms:* Place yourself (and your listeners) into the world of the story and its ancient storytellers and storylisteners. What norms of judgment about what is good and bad, right and wrong, happy and unhappy are operative? How can these values be translated in the storytelling so that they can be experienced by contemporary storylisteners? Commentaries are a primary resource for this task.

good/right/happy   *bad/wrong/unhappy*

C. *Distance:* On the basis of the shifts of perspective and norms of judgment, sense how close to or far from the characters you feel throughout the story. Does this change as the story progresses? (Can you identify modern day counterparts of the ancient characters?)

close: *far:*
(or identification with)   (or alienation from)

3. *Thought* is the expression of the story's ideas as listener expectations are built up and then reversed. It is the human decision-making of the story. Analysis of thought seeks to discover the suspense and surprise of a story's development.

   A. *Verbal Threads* are the words and phrases that are repeated in a story. They reflect the mnemonic and imaginative patterns of the original storyteller. Look for words and phrases that recur not only within the story but also across the stories that precede it (an exhaustive concordance is the key tool here). Look for associations and not definitions, for what is heightened, reversed, altered.

   B. *Diction Rules* are communication guidelines. They are applied to a story based upon analysis of plot, character, and thought.

      i. *Adapt delivery* verbally and nonverbally.

      ii. *Achieve clarity* with alternate wordings and brief explanations.

      iii. *Avoid trivialization* by keeping metaphorical terms and narrative forms.

REMEMBER: Analysis of the text is not an end in itself. It is a means to translating a written text into the spoken word!

WORKS CITED

Bailey, Kenneth E. *Poet and Peasant*. Grand Rapids, Mich.:
Eerdman's, 1976.

Bauer, Walter; F. Wilber Gingrich; and Frederick W. Danker. *A
Greek-English Lexicon of the New Testament*. 2nd ed. Chicago:
University of Chicago Press, 1979.

Eddy, Margaret R. "Life-Giving Methods of Bible Study." Unpublished doctoral demonstration project, New York Theological
Seminary, 1982.

Jeremias, Joachim. *The Parables of Jesus*. New York: Charles
Scribner's Sons, 1962.

Kittel, Gerhard, ed. *Theological Dictionary of the New Testament*. 10
vols. Grand Rapids, Mich.: Eerdman's, 1964.

Puhl, Louis J. *The Spiritual Exercises of St. Ignatius*. Chicago: Loyola
University Press, 1951.

Reicke, Bo. *The New Testament Era*. Philadelphia: Fortress, 1968.

Rhoads, David. *Israel in Revolution, 6–74 C.E.: A Political History
Based on the Writings of Josephus*. Philadelphia: Fortress, 1976.

Rhoads, David, and Donald Michie. *Mark as Story—An Introduction
to the Narrative of a Gospel*. Philadelphia: Fortress, 1982.

Wink, Walter. *Transforming Bible Study*. Nashville: Abingdon, 1980.

SELECTED BIBLIOGRAPHY

I. General

Bausch, William J. *Storytelling: Imagination and Faith*. Mystic, Conn.: Twenty-Third Publications, 1984.

Friedman, Greg. *Storytelling in Ministry*. Notre Dame, Ind.: Ave Maria Press, 1982. Audiotape.

Harrell, John, and Mary Harrell. *To Tell of Gideon: The Art of Storytelling in the Church*. Kensington, Calif.: York House, 1975.

Shea, John. The Stories of Jesus in Pastoral Ministry. Kansas City, Mo.: National Catholic Reporter, 1980. Six audiotapes.

White, William R. *Speaking in Stories: Resources for Christian Storytellers*. Minneapolis: Augsburg, 1982.

II. Foundations (Theological, Philosophical, and Historical)

Crossan, John Dominic. *The Dark Interval: Towards a Theology of Story*. Niles, Tex.: Argus Communication, 1975.

Navone, John, and Thomas Cooper. *Tellers of the Word*. New York: LeJacq Publishing, 1981.

Ong, Walter J. *Orality and Literacy: The Technologizing of the Word.* New York: Methuen, 1982.

———. *Presence of the Word: Some Prolegomena for Cultural and Religious History.* New Haven, Conn.: Yale University Press, 1967.

Tilley, Terrence W. *Story Theology.* Wilmington, Del.: Michael Glazier, 1985.

III. Media History of Biblical Narrative and Narrative Exegesis

Alter, Robert. *The Art of Biblical Narrative.* New York: Basic Books, 1981.

Bailey, Kenneth E. *Poet and Peasant.* Grand Rapids, Mich.: Eerdman's, 1976.

Culpepper, R. Alan. *Anatomy of the Fourth Gospel.* Philadelphia: Fortress, 1983.

Dibelius, Martin. *From Tradition to Gospel.* New York: Charles Scribner's Sons.

Jeremias, Joachim. *The Parables of Jesus.* New York: Charles Scribner's Sons, 1962.

Kelber, Werner H. *The Oral and Written Gospel.* Philadelphia: Fortress, 1983.

Perkins, Pheme. *Hearing the Parables of Jesus.* New York: Paulist Press, 1981.

Rhoads, David, and Donald Michie. *Mark as Story—An Introduction to the Narrative of a Gospel.* Philadelphia: Fortress, 1982.

Wilder, Amos. *Early Christian Rhetoric: The Language of the Gospel.* Cambridge, Mass.: Harvard University Press, 1971.

IV. The Art of Storytelling

Baker, Augusta, and Ellin Greene. *Storytelling: Art and Technique.* New York: Bowker, 1977.

Pellowski, Anne. *The World of Storytelling.* New York: Bowker, 1977.

Sawyer, Ruth. *The Way of the Storyteller.* New York: Penguin, 1942.

V. Preaching and Worship

Bartholomew, Gilbert L. "Narrative Preaching." *Worship Alive!* Discipleship Resources, undated publication.

Craddock, Fred B. *Overhearing the Gospel*. Nashville: Abingdon, 1978.

Jensen, Richard A. *Telling the Story: Variety and Imagination in Preaching*. Minneapolis: Augsburg, 1980.

Lee, Charlotte I. *Oral Reading of the Scriptures*. Boston: Houghton Mifflin, 1974.

Wardlaw, Don M. *Preaching Biblically: Creating Sermons in the Shape of Scripture*. Philadelphia: Westminster, 1983.

VI. Education and Biblical Study

Eddy, Margaret R. "Life-Giving Methods of Bible Study." Unpublished doctoral demonstration project, New York Theological Seminary, 1982.

Furnish, Dorothy Jean. *Living the Bible with Children*. Nashville: Abingdon, 1981.

Griggs, Patricia. *Using Storytelling in Christian Education*. Nashville: Abingdon, 1981.

Groome, Thomas H. *Christian Religious Education: Sharing Our Story and Vision*. San Francisco: Harper & Row, 1980.

Vencill, Gary. *Remember the Word*. Nashville: Graded Press, 1987.

Wink, Walter. *Transforming Bible Study*. Nashville: Abingdon, 1980.

VII. Pastoral Care and Counseling

Capps, Donald. *Biblical Approaches to Pastoral Counseling*. Philadelphia: Westminster, 1981.

VIII. Spirituality

Gill, Jean. *Images of My Self: Meditation and Self-Exploration Through the Jungian Imagery of the Gospels*. New York: Paulist Press, 1982.

Puhl, Louis J. *The Spiritual Exercises of St. Ignatius*. Chicago: Loyola University Press, 1951.

Wilhelm, Robert Bela. Storytelling for Self-Discovery. Kansas City, Mo.: National Catholic Reporter, 1977. Four audiotapes.

The address of the Network of Biblical Storytellers is 1810 Harvard Boulevard, Dayton, Ohio 45406.

INDEX

Attitude. *See* Storytelling techniques
Ancient manuscripts, 42

Characterization, distance in, 62-65, 75-76, 206
  alienation, 76-80, 87-88, 126, 148, 162-63, 168-69
  identification, 88-90, 97-98, 183-84
  judgment, 114
  names, 125-26, 161-62, 182-83
Connections, 15-16, 36-38, 65-66, 98-103, 116-19, 128-30, 150-51, 170-75, 188-94
  appropriate, 20-21, 169
  between biblical stories and our stories, 20-21
  communal experiences, 37-38
  darkness, 90-91, 188
  personal experiences, 36-37
Covenant, 143, 146-53

Education
  adults, 153-58
  community formation, 155-58
  memorization/internalization, 153-58
  Suzuki method, 157
Enemies, 110-12, 115-16, 119
Episodes, 24, 27-28, 74-75, 206
  as scenes, 46-47, 59-60, 110
  beginnings, 28, 46-47
Experiential Bible study, 10, 129-31

Learning biblical stories, 23
  alone, 21, 23-31
  chunking, 29
  images, 28
  internalization, 43-44
  structure, 24, 27-28, 46
  with a partner, 44-46
Listener, 52, 147, 181

Martyrdom
  of Isaiah, 166
  of seven boys (II Maccabees), 110-12, 165, 167

213

Index

Memory
  ancient world, 41-42
  head, heart, and gut, 43-44, 49, 60
  memorization techniques, 28-31, 44-47, 53-59
  word for word vs. improvisation, 31
Methods of biblical study
  communal exegesis, 10, 129-31
  form criticism, 60-65
  See also Narrative/literary criticism

Narrative commentary, 75, 96, 168-69, 182-82, 186
Narrative/literary criticism, 10
  categories, 73-76, 205-7
Narrative point of view, 35, 41, 47, 74-75, 207
  inside views, 79-85, 88, 97-98, 126, 183-86
Network of Biblical Storytellers, 10, 11, 104, 201
Norms of judgment, 35, 75, 87-90, 113-14, 166-67, 186-88, 206

Oral narrative, characteristics of
  emphasis, 26-27, 34, 161-62
  repetitions, 163. *See also* Verbal threads
  tempo, 26, 35, 85, 181
  tone, 48, 86, 97-98, 126, 167, 183
  volume, 98

Personal experiences
  battle of the bell, 174-75
  bicycle crash, 101-2
  burying the pen, 193-94
  forgetting turkey dinner, 118-19
  getting a scared boy to sleep, 156
  journey up the river, 15-16

learning to walk again, 67-68
  the panther, 100-101
Plot, 74, 163-64, 168, 182, 205
  climax of Mark, 185-86
  reversals, 170, 184, 188
Prayer, 11, 51, 105-6, 199

Religious experience
  commissionings, 50-51, 181
  discipleship, 123
  fear, 93-105
  forgiveness, 53, 63, 64-67, 83-84, 87-89
  healing, 67-68, 108
  naming, 82, 125-26
  peace, 189-91
  repentance, 80-82, 88-92
  suffering, 170-75

Sermon
  Bartimaeus, 135-41
  outline as story, 133-35
Stories about storytelling in ministry
  agoraphobia, 103-4
  boy in hospital, 39-40
  holocaust in Latvia, 171-73
  recital of passion narrative, 176-77
  resurrection peace, 189-91
  the sower and rebuilding Broadway United Methodist Church, 195-96
  walking on the water and West End Collegiate, 104-5
Storytelling
  and peacemaking, 120-21
  as a journey, 15-16, 197-98
  as primary language of the church, 202
  characteristics of, 18-19
  gospel as, 16
  in Israel and early Christianity, 19-20

Storytelling techniques
  attitude, 34, 62-63, 110
  gestures, 76
  tempo, 26, 34-35, 85, 182
  tone, 48, 86, 97-98, 126
  volume, 98
Teaching the stories
  blab school, 58-59
  in religious education, 153-58
  lion hunt, 50-51
  preparation, 54
  story theater, 117
  to others, 198-201
Telling the story, 52, 91-92, 199-200
  in mission, 194-96
  in relation to covenant, 152-53
  in relation to fear, 103-6
  in religious education, 153-55
  in social witness, 119-21
  in worship, 131-41, 176-77

  to a partner, 66-67
  to yourself, 67-68
Trusting the story, 195

Using storytelling in ministry
  Eucharist, 151-53
  pastoral care, 66-67, 105-6
  peacemaking, 120-21
  preaching, 133-34
  scripture lesson, 131-33
  social action, 107, 114
  worship, 131-34, 151-53, 176-77

Verbal threads, 27, 33-34, 46, 59-60, 71-72, 76, 94-95, 108-9, 124-25, 148, 161-62, 169, 181-82, 207
  to Old Testament stories, 48, 127

SCRIPTURE INDEX

Genesis
2–3.................................9
3:10.............................186
8:8-12.............................48
15:1...............................96
19:1-11..........................147
19:8..............................147
26:28-30........................147
31:43-54........................147
41:42..............................84

Exodus
3:6................................82
3:14..............................96
3:46.............................186
22:8-9............................82
24:8.............................149
33:19.............................96
33:22.............................96
34:20.............................82
34:23.............................82

Numbers
6:1-4............................150
22:21-35........................186

Joshua
2–3, 6...........................130

Judges
6:23..............................96
13:4-5...........................150
19...............................147
19:23............................147
19, 20...........................147

I Samuel
1:11.............................150
9–10..............................48
16................................48

II Samuel
6:6-7............................186
11:1-4...........................149
11:11............................149
21:4-5...........................149
14:33.............................83

I Kings
19:5-8............................49

Scripture Index

I Kings (continued)
19:11............................96
2..............................130
2:8............................130
2:2-14.........................130
2:9............................130
2:9-10.........................127
5..............................110
13:20-32.......................147

Psalms
6:2............................126
9:13...........................126
22...................114, 163, 167
22:7...........................165
22:12-13.......................114
22:16..........................114
22:19..........................163
22:20-21.......................114
30:10..........................126
41:4...........................126
86:3...........................126

Job
16:4...........................165

Isaiah
5:1-14.........................166
61:10...........................84

Daniel
6...............................48
7–8.............................48
9:22-23.........................49
10:11...........................49
10:12...........................96
18–19...........................49

Amos
2:11-12........................150

Sirach
12:18..........................165
13:7...........................165

I Maccabees
2..............................32
II Maccabees
6–7.......................110, 113

Matthew
6:12............................89
9:36............................44
14:14...........................44
14:22...........................95
14:22-23..................95, 103
14:22-33...................93-94
14:23...........................95
18:23-35........................89
14:24...........................95
14:25...........................95
14:26......................94, 95
14:27...........................95
14:28...........................95
14:29...........................95
14:30...........................95
14:31-32........................95
14:31-33........................95
14:32...........................95
22:15-22........................32

Mark
1:9............................48
1:9-13.........................43
1:11...........................48
1:12...........................48
1:41...........................44
1:45..........................188
2:1-2..........................61
2:1-13......................56-57
2:4............................64
2:5..............59, 66, 86, 128
2:6........................59, 62
2:7............................61
2:8............................59
2:9............................59
2:10...........................62
2:11...........................59
2:12...........................59
2:21...........................84
3:8...........................110
3:11..........................169

Mark (continued)

4:35	145
4:41	186
5:7	169
5:15	186
5:21-23	109
5:22	113
5:25-34	115
5:33	128, 186
5:34	128
5:35-43	109
5:36	128
6:3	169
6:6	128
6:26	146
6:41	145, 148
6:50	186
6:52	148
7:1-23	113
7:24-30	107-8
7:26	96, 108, 113
7:27	108, 109
7:28	108, 109
7:29	108
7:30	108
8:6	145, 148
8:17-21	148
8:31	182
8:31-33	130
8:33	130
9:7	169
9:23	128
9:31	182
9:36-37	109
10:13-16	109
10:34	182
10:35-37	127
10:36	130
10:37	164
10:40	164
10:46-52	123-24
10:47	124, 126
10:48	124, 126
10:49	125, 126
10:50	126
10:51	125, 126, 130

10:52	125
11:11	145
12:13-17	32
14:10	145
14:10-11	145
14:12-16	146
14:17	144
14:17-25	143-44
14:18	144, 145, 146
14:20	144, 145
14:21	144, 145
14:22	144, 148
14:22-23	145, 162
14:28	185
14:50	185
14:51	183
14:52	185
14:57-58	165
14:61	165
14:61-62	164
14:62	183
14:66-71	182
14:68	182
14:70-71	182
15:2	156, 165
15:2-9	165
15:15	167
15:20	162
15:21-41	159-61
15:23	162
15:24	161, 163
15:24-25	168
15:25	161
15:25-26	163
15:27	161, 164
15:29-32	164
15:31-32	161
15:32	161
15:33	165, 183
15:34	161, 167
15:35-36	162
15:37	161
15:40-41	169
15:42	182

Mark (continued)
15:47.............................. 184
16:1..................................183
16:1-8............................. 180
16:2..........................181, 183
16:3..........................181, 183
16:4..........................181, 183
16:5.................. 181, 183, 184
16:6..................................181
16:7..................................185
16:8................. 181, 185, 186

Luke
1:13...................................96
1:29-30............................184
1:39-56.............................. 33
2.. 33
2:1-5.................................. 27
2:1-20..........................25-26,
2:3.....................................26
2:4.....................................33
2:4-5...........................26, 34
2:5.....................................27
2:7............................. 27, 33
2:9............................. 26, 33
2:10.................... 26, 96, 184
2:11.............................26, 27
2:12.................................. 27
2:13.................................. 27
2:14.................................. 34
2:16.................................. 27
2:17-18.............................. 27
2:18-20.............................. 34
2:20.................................. 27
5:17.................................. 62
5:17-26.............................. 61

7:15-25............................. 85
12:17................................80
15:11-12...........................76
15:11-32.......................69-71
15:15-16...........................79
15:17-19...........................80
15:18................................71
15:20-21...........................83
15:21................................71
15:22-24...........................84
15:23................................72
15:24....................... 71, 72
15:25....................... 72, 85
15:26-27...........................85
15:27................................72
15:28....................... 72, 85
15:29-30...........................86
15:30................................72
15:31-32...........................86
15:32................................71
16:3.................................. 80
20:16.............................. 126
20:20-26............................32
24:13-32.......................... 198

Acts
6–7..................................187
21–23..............................187
24:14.............................. 131

Revelation
4:4....................................84
7:9....................................84
7:14.................................. 84
22:14................................84

Story Journey:
An Invitation to the
Gospel as Storytelling

Audiocassettes

The heart of a story is in the telling and the hearing.
Abingdon Press presents Tom Boomershine, nationally
known storyteller, author, and biblical scholar, on
audiocassette.

Now, you can hear, share, and enjoy the Gospel stories
from **Story Journey,** plus additional related biblical stories,
as told by Tom. Also included are six sessions in which
Tom guides you on your own journey into the Gospels.
You will discover how to tell your own faith story, and
venture into the authentic way the gospel was originally
proclaimed—by sharing the story of Jesus and his
ministry.

Listen, learn, and enjoy these story tapes at home, at work,
in your car, or while you jog!

- These two ninety-minute audiocassettes are a conve-
  nient and easy way for pastors to learn narrative
  preaching and the authentic Gospel stories.
- Those who are hospitalized or shut-in can experience
  God's presence through Tom's telling of the stories of
  Jesus' ministry.
- Bible study groups and church school classes (youth to
  adult) will discover how to hear and tell the stories of
  Jesus' life and ministry in a way that is historically and
  personally authentic.

Both tapes *(ninety minutes each)* for only **$12.95.**
Available at your local bookstore.   **ISBN** 0-687-76026-7